CUSTOM MADE WOMAN

American Music: New Roots

David Menconi, editor

Featuring work by journalists, music critics, scholars, and musicians themselves, this series aims to expand and challenge the way we think about American roots music genres, traditions, performers, and their ever-expanding contributions. Books in the series not only bring new perspective on familiar roots traditions like jazz, the blues, country, and folk music but also offer fundamentally new ways to consider where the roots of today's American music lie, what stories are told about them, and who does the telling.

A complete list of books published in American Music: New Roots is available at https://uncpress.org/series/american-music-new-roots/.

ALICE GERRARD

The University of North Carolina Press
CHAPEL HILL

This book was published with the assistance of the Greensboro Women's Fund of the University of North Carolina Press. Founding contributors: Linda Arnold Carlisle, Sally Schindel Cone, Anne Faircloth, Bonnie McElveen Hunter, Linda Bullard Jennings, Janice J. Kerley (in honor of Margaret Supplee Smith), Nancy Rouzer May, and Betty Hughes Nichols.

All photographs by Alice Gerrard unless otherwise noted.
Manufactured in the United States of America

Designed and typeset by Lindsay Starr in Latienne URW.

Cover art courtesy Alice Gerrard.

Library of Congress Cataloging-in-Publication Data
Names: Gerrard, Alice, 1934- author
Title: Custom made woman : a life in traditional music / Alice Gerrard.
Other titles: American music: new roots
Description: Chapel Hill : The University of North Carolina Press, 2025. | Series: American music: new roots
Identifiers: LCCN 2025026053 | ISBN 9781469690360 cloth alk. paper | ISBN 9781469683331 epub | ISBN 9781469690377 pdf
Subjects: LCSH: Gerrard, Alice, 1934- | Folk musicians—United States—Biography | Women folk musicians—United States—Biography | Bluegrass musicians—United States—Biography | Women bluegrass musicians—United States—Biography | BISAC: MUSIC / Ethnomusicology | MUSIC / Genres & Styles / Folk & Traditional | LCGFT: Autobiographies
Classification: LCC ML420.G3686 A3 2025 | DDC 782.42162/130092 [B]—dc23/eng/20250613
LC record available at https://lccn.loc.gov/2025026053

For product safety concerns under the European Union's General Product Safety Regulation (EU GPSR), please contact gpsr@mare-nostrum.co.uk or write to the University of North Carolina Press and Mare Nostrum Group B.V., Mauritskade 21D, 1091 GC Amsterdam, The Netherlands.

CONTENTS

Sidebars

CUSTOM MADE WOMAN

Dedicated to my children, Cory, Jenny, Joel, and Jesse Foster, and all of our wonderful extended family, and to all of the many musicians, here and gone, who have inspired me and shared their music and lives.

INTRODUCTION

How It All Began

"Here, listen to this," said my college friend Jeremy Foster, as he handed me his copy of the *Harry Smith Anthology of American Folk Music*, the six-LP set put out in 1952 by Folkways Records. It was a powerful moment for me that resonated for the rest of my life (so far)—the sounds of the banjo, blues, guitars, fiddles, and the voices . . . oh those voices! I wanted to learn this music, I wanted to sing like that, I wanted to play like that!

I started to teach myself the guitar and the banjo. I haunted the Antioch College music library, which happened to have a 78 rpm recording of the great traditional singer from Saltville, Virginia, Texas Gladden, singing "One Morning in May." Her powerful, mournful voice tells a woman's version of the better-known song "Streets of Laredo," this time from the experience of a prostitute who is suffering from disease and dying, whose body is "salvating," yearning for her mama and papa, and wanting four young ladies each to carry a bunch of white roses to lay on her coffin "as I pass along." The song starts in the prostitute's voice and ends in the voice of a bystander: "One morning in May, I spied this young lady all wrapped in white linen, as cold as the clay."

Transported into the song by the wrenching mournfulness of the singer's voice, I could feel the alienation, the desperate need for comfort, the profound sadness of the story. And it spoke to me, resonating deeply with many of my own feelings. My father had died when I was young, and I think that when a child loses a parent at a young age, there forms inside a reservoir of sadness that no matter how life goes on, remains in some form at your core. Maybe that child is always searching for family, truth, connectedness, community, authenticity. . . . The music I was hearing spoke to all those things, and I decided that somehow, in some form, this music would be in my life.

Listening to the *Harry Smith Anthology* changed my life. Instead of heading down paths of more popular folk music that led to Susan Reed, the Kingston Trio, Joan Baez, and Judy Collins, I took the road less traveled with my companions Clarence Ashley, G. B. Grayson, the Carter Family, Sleepy John Estes, Dock Boggs, the Memphis Sanctified Singers, Richard "Rabbit" Brown, Ernest and Hattie Stoneman, and others. And I never really left that road.

Follow the Music

Since I was a child I been a-lookin for a home
Been everywhere and I been nowhere at all
Thought it was a place, thought I saw it in your face
& sometimes in the comfort of a lover's warm embrace.

So I'm out in this old world just a-ramblin around
Ramblin in the country, ramblin in the town
Followin the river, cross the ocean deep and wide
Stars stretchin out for miles keep me thru the night

Follow the music
Follow the music home
Follow the music home

Sometimes in the night I hear a lonesome old song
Or a ghostly fiddle calling, where you been so long
(And) if I follow the music to where I want to go
It'll take me to safe harbor and guide me home

—*Follow the Music*

Tucked away in nooks and crannies throughout the country live(d) countless banjo players, fiddlers, singers, guitar players. . . . Going to visit them, listening to their stories, eating and playing music with them, learning about their lives, has always been one of the great joys and sidebars to my musical life. In the best of circumstances, you got to go back again and again, but sometimes it was fleeting—a one-off—but nevertheless memorable. If it was mealtime, "Come on and eat with us," and invariably "Let's have a tune." And over time, you might become a part of their lives—an exchange of music, ideas, laughter or tears, food, help when needed. . . . It was never a one-way street. I visited a lot of traditional musicians over the years, not only in Galax, Virginia, but many other parts of the South (mostly), and I remember those visits and think back now and realize how amazingly lucky I was to have had that chance.

WHERE'D SHE COME FROM, WHERE'D SHE GO?

I'm a musician, songwriter, twice a wife, four times a mother, a sister, once widowed and once divorced. I grew up on the West Coast in a musical family. My mother and her seven sisters and brothers grew up on a fruit ranch near Yakima, Washington. The girls were all singers and players of classical music and toured for a brief while as the Symphony Sisters Quartette.

My father was from England—a Lancashire boy, fifteen when he ran away from his home near Wigan in 1905. He somehow wrangled a job as a deck boy on one of the last of the three-masted schooners, the ship *Bardowie* (they named my brother Philip Bardowie Gerrard after the ship), leaving from South Shields near Newcastle, England, carrying coke, pig iron, and firebrick, and arriving in San Francisco in 1906. It took them a year to get to San Francisco, and another month to sail to Astoria, Oregon, during which time the 1906 San Francisco earthquake happened. Family history has it that my father jumped ship in Astoria, thus starting his life in America, moving eventually to Seattle. He loved to sing sea chanteys around the house, and I remember bits and pieces: "Can she bake a cherry pie / Billy boy, Billy boy. . . ."; "What'll we do with the drunken sailor . . . early in the morning. . . ."; "Give me some time to blow the man down." He had a fine, strong voice. It still rings out in my memory.

I grew up with music and singing in the house all the time. A get-together wasn't about cocktails and chitchat; it was about sharing music. Musical friends and relatives of my parents came over and everyone played music. I don't remember much about what they played and sang, but what stayed with me was the sense of homemade music, of having fun playing music with friends, laughing and having a good time. I used to sneak down and sit on the stairs at night when I was supposed to be in bed, listening, taking note.

My father was a joyful person from what I remember—taking me out at night before I went to bed to say goodnight to the big madrona tree in the front yard; holding me up to the window during a thunder and lightning storm to be awestruck, instead of afraid. But he became ill with heart disease and my mother suffered a lot with rheumatoid arthritis, and sickness became a menacing presence living in the house with us. A lot of my memories of Seattle are dark and sad. My father died when I was about eight, and my mother, brother, and I moved to Guadalajara, Mexico, for a year and then to Alameda County, California, to a farm near Irvington in southern Alameda County, where we settled during our elementary and middle-school years. I was horse crazy as well as dog crazy, constantly begging to have a horse. I'd wake up every Christmas morning thinking, "This is the morning there'll be a horse waiting for me outside."

It never happened just that way, but my mother did an amazing thing when she arranged for me to hang out with the foreman on a nearby cattle ranch. I followed Mateo around like a puppy dog, spending every waking moment that I didn't have to go to school, riding with him, working cattle with him; he showed me how to take care of a horse, and eventually my mother got me a horse that I named Dusty. Dusty and I spent long days together

Me at six or seven years old, wishing I was on that horse. Courtesy Alice Gerrard.

riding around the countryside, all up and down the wild brown hills (at that time empty of "progress") that rose over the bay and farmlands of Alameda County. I'd take my lunch and we'd just go. Happiest days.

This early experience inspired my song "Quiero Decir Gracias a Mateo":

I was just a little skinny girl out California way
Turned up my nose at baby dolls, play house and fancy clothes
All I wanted in the whole world was to ride the western range
And to count myself a friend to Mateo.
Oh he was a cowboy come up from Mexico
I never asked him how or why he came
But the days I spent there by his side were the happiest days of all
Y quiero decir gracias a Mateo. . . .

Shortly after World War II, my mother married Willard Rosenquist, an artist who taught at the University of California, Berkeley, and it made sense to them to move to Oakland to be closer to his work. I joined the throngs at Oakland Technical High School and reluctantly became a city girl. I listened to the popular music of the day and was drawn to the slightly more weird and mysterious songs, like Frankie Laine's "Wild Goose," Nat King Cole's "Nature Boy," or the different sounds of the harpsichord with Rosemary Clooney and "Come On-a My House." I felt alienated, out of place—it was the late 1940s, early '50s, and my teenage life was playing out against the political backdrop of McCarthyism, loyalty oaths, liberal California congresswoman Helen Gahagan Douglas versus Richard Nixon, crackdowns on suspected communists, smear and fear campaigns (sound familiar?), etc. My mother had joined a progressive political group, the United World Federalists, and at some point she gave me some raffle tickets to sell, to help raise money for the UWF. I took them to high school and the general reaction from the few students I approached was "Don't you know that's a communist organization?" I was mortified.

I was never one of the "popular" kids, but I found some comfort and sense of belonging when I joined the youth group at the Berkeley Unitarian Church, where my parents had become members. They were a wonderful group, these kids—also misfits to some extent, a gaggle of talented young people who liked to folk dance and were into liberal politics. I was impressed in particular with a gangly, skinny young guy with big ears, Ron Riddle, a piano player originally from Kentucky, who could play by ear and was a wonderful ragtime player.

After I graduated from high school in 1952, the family (which now included my half-brother Elan) all took off for Europe during my stepfather's sabbatical year. My brother Philip and I were set free to roam—youth-hosteling, hitchhiking, and biking everywhere. Every so often we'd check in with the parents who were on their own trip, but essentially we were on our own. It was an amazing time. I don't think many parents would have turned their kids loose to such an extent, but whether it was consciously thought out as an educational/growth strategy or simply "ignorance is bliss," it was wonderful!

I never looked much beyond the present as we traveled around Europe and was probably thinking in some vague way that I would just stay on, fall in love, and live happily ever after on the shores of Mallorca, continuing my occasional babysitting jobs taking care of Timothy Leary's kids (yes, *the* Tim Leary—he lived down the hill from the house we'd rented). I did fall in love (several times), but much to my parents' relief didn't end up on the beach or become the Learys' nanny, or marry the handsome streetcar conductor I had a crush on. Somehow I applied to (with much prodding by parents I'm sure) and was accepted at a small liberal arts college, Antioch, in Yellow Springs, Ohio. Leaving Europe felt like the end of everything as far as I was concerned. I think I dreaded going back to my "life as I knew it." The boat docked in New York, my family drove back to California and dropped me off at Antioch on the way. I'll never forget my first view of the campus—beards, sandals, people sitting around under trees playing guitars, singing—not so very different from Europe. It was 1953 and I felt like I had arrived home.

During the couple of years I spent at Antioch I let my emotions and sense of discipline run free or amok, depending. I paid less attention to academics and more attention to friends—running around on the field behind my dorm in a thunderstorm, oblivious to the prospect of lightning strikes, hanging out at Com's, a local restaurant owned by an African American couple, Goldie and Com. They made the best pork chop sandwich I've ever had—fried, bone-in, between two slices of white bread with mayo. I can still taste it. And there was this great new music I was trying to learn, teaching myself guitar and banjo.

I had no idea what I wanted to do with my life, never thought about a career, just kind of went along, a little of this and a little of that. Like many other women in the 1950s, I grew up assuming I'd end up married; my husband would work and I would stay home and take care of the kids and household. No need to worry about a career!

Then there was love. While falling in love with the music, I was falling in love with Jeremy, a charismatic physics major who loved traditional

Practicing the guitar, Washington, DC, ca. 1961.
Photo by Jeremy Foster; courtesy Alice Gerrard.

music. He was tall, dark, smart, and somewhat exotic, wearing a full-length cape the first time I saw him. . . . Music and love. A powerful combination. Antioch required that students take co-op jobs (internships) to graduate, and both Jeremy and I chose Washington, DC, because of its proximity to music and musicians, like our friends Mike Seeger, West Virginia singer Hazel Dickens and her family, Pete Kuykendall (musician and future cofounder of the magazine *Bluegrass Unlimited*), record collector Dick Spottswood, and a host of others who were immersing themselves in the lively interchange between traditional musicians who had moved up from the South and young kids like us who were their eager acolytes.

Jeremy was about to flunk out of Antioch as a physics major in part due to family pressure, real or imagined, to measure up to his grandfather, Nobel laureate physicist Albert A. Michelson. Jeremy decided he'd rather drop out than flunk out, and in the mid-1950s to drop out meant the draft. He was sent to Fort Jackson in Columbia, South Carolina, for basic training, I continued at Antioch for a while, then dropped out as well. I wasn't bent toward academia and had no particular plan beyond music and hanging with my boyfriend and all our musician friends. Mike Seeger and I traveled to Columbia, South Carolina, in 1956 to visit Jeremy while he was in basic training, and also to see DeWitt "Snuffy" Jenkins, who lived there and was performing on the army base. Jenkins was a three-finger-style banjo player and medicine show performer who was a great influence on many bluegrass musicians, including Don Reno and Earl Scruggs. Mike wanted to record him for the *American Banjo: Three-Finger and Scruggs Style* Folkways LP he was putting together.

Mike was a young musician and budding recording engineer—a skinny, bright, somewhat socially awkward boy who had grown up in a musical family. Mike learned to play at a young age surrounded by countless recordings of traditional music and by the enthusiasm and

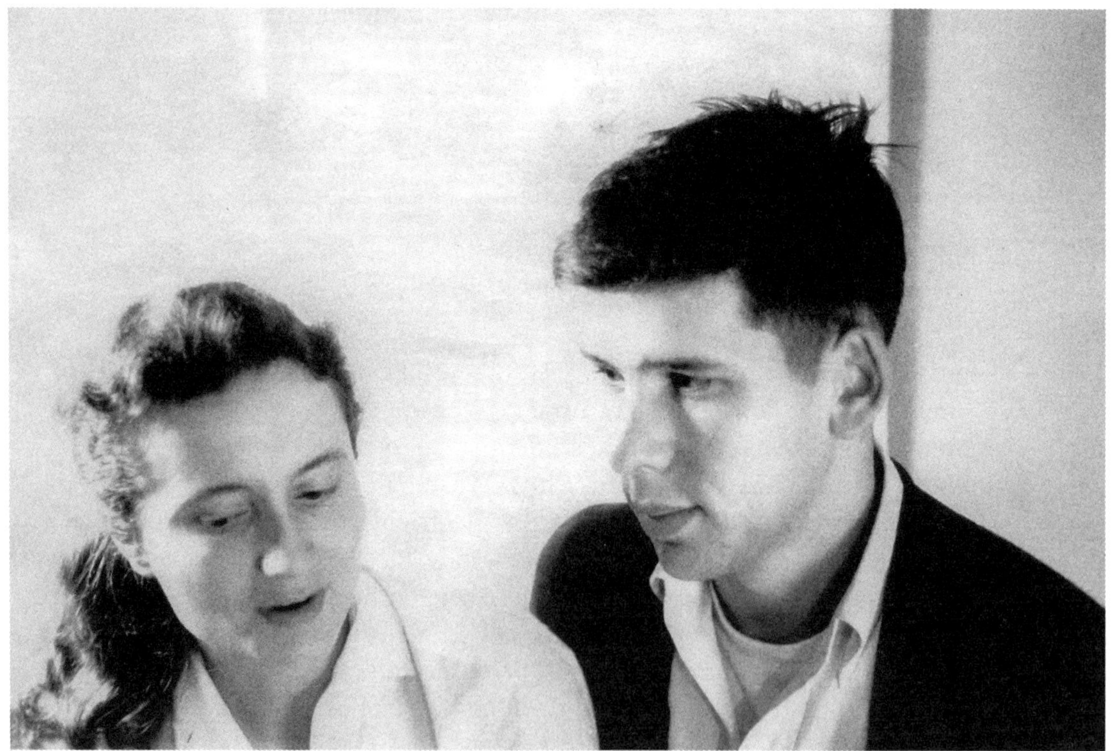

Jeremy used to take photos of the two of us. He would set up the camera and timer. There were a bunch, but I particularly like this ca. 1957 one. Photo by Jeremy Foster; courtesy Alice Gerrard.

Mike Seeger and Hazel Dickens,
Washington, DC, 1969.

work of his parents, Ruth Crawford Seeger and Charles Seeger, classical musicians who were also active field collectors and transcribers of American folk music during the Works Progress Administration New Deal years of the 1930s. The Seegers wrote or coauthored several well-known collections of songs and tunes based on their field recordings: *Our Singing Country*, *Folk Song USA*, and *American Folk Songs for Children*. It was Mike and his sister, Peggy, who discovered that the woman who worked as a domestic in their home, Elizabeth Cotten, was a great guitarist and banjoist. ("Libba," as the Seegers called her, was later to garner worldwide fame and accolades as a touring musician, recording artist, and songwriter ("Freight Train," among others), inducted into the Rock 'n' Roll Hall of Fame in 2022—beloved by all.)

In ways both direct and indirect, Mike Seeger was a huge influence on all of us during the early 1950s, and later in my life as well. Jeremy and Mike had attended the same high school, and Jeremy often hung out at Mike's home in Northwest Washington, DC. He dated Mike's sister, Peggy, for a while and became interested in traditional music through Mike and his family. During the Korean War of the early 1950s, Mike was working as a conscientious objector in the Mount Wilson Tuberculosis Sanitorium in Pikesville, Maryland, outside of Baltimore, where Hazel Dickens's brother Robert was a patient. It was this connection that led first to Mike's, then Jeremy's, and ultimately to my meeting Hazel. Lots of tangled, diverse paths, and connections, leading to wonderful friendships and lives lived in music. Pretty amazing!

Jeremy and I married in 1956 and had our first child, Cora Lee, shortly after that. When Jeremy's army stint ended, we went back to Antioch (now with a small child) so he could finish up with a degree in mathematics, and there we had our second child, Jenny. When Jeremy graduated in 1961, we moved back to what was now our home base, Washington, DC, where we had two more children, Joel and Jesse.

Besides playing music, Jeremy and Mike, and others, were part of the underground of people who were passing around and sharing old recordings and tapes, mining the collections of DC friend and record collector Dick Spottswood; Joe Bussard, another record collector from up around Frederick, Maryland; and others. (I remember hearing about how Mike and Ralph Rinzler used to sneak field recordings out of the New York Public Library and copy them—or was it the Library of Congress—I forget which.) I was never much of a true collector, but I took good advantage of the bounty of music they collected via tape recordings, old 78s, and more. It's hard to know how many amazing recordings they may have saved from dumpsters or trash heaps, caring for them and passing along the music to those who were interested. One year for my birthday, Jeremy copied every Blue Sky Boys recording from Pete Kuykendall's collection. The Blue Sky Boys were two brothers, Bill and Earl Bolick (d. 1998 and 2008, respectively), from Hickory, North Carolina, who had recorded a lot and were popular during the 1930s and sporadically into the 1970s. I still love those Blue Sky Boys harmonies—their gentle voices, swaying, gliding, tightly enmeshed—a sound that families, brothers, sisters, mothers, and daughters can have naturally, and others strive for.

Enthusiasts (often musicians) who loved the sounds from these varied collections started looking for the artists, realizing they might still be alive and still playing music. I remember the time that Dick Spottswood came running through the front door shouting that Tom Hoskins had "found" Mississippi John Hurt and was going to record him; Sara and Maybelle Carter were living and still playing! Sam Charters had "found" Lightnin' Hopkins and recorded him in 1959.

In 1963 Mike Seeger's wife, Marge, had the obvious and brilliant idea that Dock Boggs might be listed in the Norton, Virginia, phone directory. They were in the area, she looked him up and there he was! Suddenly these legendary musicians were real, many of them still playing as they always had, in the communities where they lived. People like Mike, Tom, Sam, and others began to encourage them to "come out" and let them know that a lot of people would be interested and excited to hear them play. They were presented to enthusiastic Northern audiences at folk festivals and concerts.

I believe it was in 1959 that I visited the Highlander Folk School in Monteagle, Tennessee. It happened that Guy Carawan, folksinger and activist, was on his way to Highlander and en route visited Antioch, showing films and speaking about his "illegal" trip to China with Peggy Seeger. At an informal music session with him, he suggested that my friend DeeDee Halleck and I go with him to Highlander since he was headed that way.

Always a controversial center, "a training ground for communists," as some called it, Highlander was founded in 1932 by Myles Horton, Don West, and Jim Dombrowski to serve as a center for social justice, training in nonviolence, antisegregation, union and civil rights organizing. It was host, over the years, to a multitude of activists including Martin Luther King Jr., Rosa Parks, Septima Clark, Pete Seeger, John Lewis, Eleanor Roosevelt, and Bernice Reagon, among many others. It was my first close look at civil rights in the South. We all sat around and they talked to us about the school, its work, and about local attempts to bomb Highlander, create fear around it, and shut it down. Myles was very interested in the idea of involving local traditional musicians to help break down barriers, transcend them, and help bring communities together through traditional music. Much the same idea as when a decade later Anne Romaine and Bernice Reagon founded the Southern tours that became the Southern Folk Cultural Project. Our visit to Highlander took place before Tennessee shuttered them and sold off the land and property. Not to be kept down, they reorganized immediately and opened in 1961 in Knoxville as the Highlander Research and Education Center, moving to New Market, Tennessee, in 1971. I remember clearly the evening we sat on the porch of the old place in Monteagle, talking. Many of the details are blurry, but the impact was sharp and strong.

I've had a longtime love affair with traditional music—old-time, country, roots, whatever you want to call it—for over seventy years. Documentation was never my first goal, music was. Like so many others who were discovering this musical world, I developed a love for it by hearing it and meeting the people who played and sang the music. I wanted to learn this music—not to develop a career but because, like so many others, I loved it. I had a need to understand not only the music but its context, the everyday of it, the politics of it; to understand cultures different from my own. Who were these people who made such beautiful music? Often going into their homes and communities, sometimes out of our comfort zones, we learned from them and became friends. Music almost always transcended barriers.

What was so compelling about this music to young people who didn't grow up with it? I think that there was a comfort of sorts in the sense of place, of tradition, of story, the sense of kinship and ritual that the music held and that we felt was perhaps missing from our lives. This was and is "outsider" music, rooted in a folk tradition where ideally you help your neighbor, express feelings about injustice, politics, love, longing for the homeplace, and where you value your ties to kin and culture—a music not overtaken by corporate America. And these were concepts that many young, middle-class "hippies" like myself were attracted to. Along the way we recorded the music by whatever means possible (usually determined by what we could afford in the way of equipment and tape), and took pictures, somehow knowing it was important.

PICTURE THIS

I don't remember being particularly interested in photography, although there is an old photo of my father with a maybe-eight-year-old me holding what looks like an old Brownie camera. I think I am something of an observer. As a child, left in the car to wait for my mother while she'd do some shopping, I'd often kill time and amuse myself by watching people—what they were doing, their mannerisms, appearance, making up stories about them. There were no cell phones then, or Facebook or Twitter. Just observation, imagination, and slow time. I can still zone out in a restaurant if I'm sitting by myself, and watch people—"Why aren't they talking to one another?" "That guy is trying too hard," "That girl really doesn't want to be with her mom," etc.—making up unlikely scenarios in my mind. Maybe they watch me too.

Most of the photos of my early married and family life in the mid-1950s to early '60s were taken by Jeremy with an old family camera. He loved his children, and he took loads of pictures of them. We were married for only seven years, and suddenly in 1964 he was killed in a

Me showing Cory how to put picks on her fingers in order to play bluegrass-style banjo, Washington, DC, 1961. Photo by Jeremy Foster; courtesy Alice Gerrard.

car crash on his way to work. Many years have passed since then, and when I think back on that time I remember the sadness, anger, chaos, loneliness, overwhelming feelings of *What am I going to do now?*; the memory of the fight we'd had that morning before he left, and the guilt, the reality of four children under the age of seven, now without a father they adored, who did fun and interesting things with them. And there was the comfort of friends who rallied around and supported us through the dark times then and to come.

I was lucky in that I was able to receive maximum Social Security (Thank you, Franklin Roosevelt!!) and a settlement from the accident. If I was frugal, I wouldn't have to worry about getting a job that would support me and four kids, which saved us since I had no kind of training of any kind in any field, and no college degree. When I became interested in photography as a hobby, I could afford the time to "mess around," taking pictures and experimenting a bit, taking a short course offered by the Smithsonian. I bought a Federal enlarger and started printing my own pictures using my small bathroom as a darkroom. I'd set boards across the sink and bathtub and set out the enlarger and trays of chemicals. The tub served as a wash. My children were often subjects in my trials and errors. I made do, and it worked.

Time passed and through it all music and kids' voices were the soundtrack to my life. And there were friends. Trails were beginning to form in the tangled underbrush of my life. Perhaps a map, a goal, or at least a plan would present itself. Through Mike and Jeremy, I had earlier met, become friends with, and begun a musical partnership with Hazel Dickens. This partnership took on greater urgency as we were encouraged to think in terms of actually performing, forming a band and getting some work. And through Jeremy and Mike in particular, I learned the value of documentation.

I moved a lot between 1965 and 1989, and my tapes, photos, and negatives got dragged around with me—no climate control and lots of disorganization. Sometimes I kept good records, most of the time I did not.

Those photos, most of which were taken between 1965 and 1990, are the inspiration for this book. Tom Rankin and Charlie Thompson of the Center for Documentary Studies at Duke University encouraged and hired this college dropout to teach one semester as the Lehman Brady Visiting Professor. Fortunately, Mike Taylor (a musician, folklore graduate student, and later the founding member of the indie rock band Hiss Golden Messenger) became my grad student assistant, helping me to find my way through the academic maze. Teaching at the center enabled me to use their equipment to start digitizing my long-neglected negatives. Occasionally other photographers at the center would stop to see what I was doing as I scanned negative after negative, staring at the computer screen with the black-and-white images bringing back so many memories. Occasionally someone would comment on a photo, and I believe it was Tom Rankin who actually said something like, "You should do a book."

Somewhat overwhelmed by the number of photographs and uncertainty about how to organize it all, I've arranged this book into "chapters" or sections that reflect various times in my life that were important to me. Most of the photos were taken by me, a few by others. I have many people to thank who've encouraged and helped me along the way. Over the years this book has been shoved onto the back burner, subject to my life as a musician—touring, rehearsing, taking on other music and music-related projects; my life with my children; my life with grandchildren; my life with dogs; aging and having less energy—and myriad other necessary distractions and circumstances. But eventually I came back to this book and knew I wanted to see it in the world.

Chapter 1

LIKE A BLIND HOG STUMBLED ON AN ACORN

College dropouts like Jeremy were subject to the draft, and drafted he was. He finished his basic training in South Carolina and in 1957 was assigned to what once was Fort Monmouth in New Jersey. We lived in a second-floor rental near the base, and I—it wasn't "we" back then—was about to give birth to our first child, Cora Lee, whom we would call Cory. Our time there wasn't very memorable, except for two images that I'll never forget—the days spent at the nearby beach, swimming and lying face down in the sand with a hole dug out for my pregnant belly; and our hefty landlady sitting in her small glassed-in sun porch watching the world go by and amusing herself by smooshing flies against the glass with her bare thumb.

Cory's birth was an army hospital birth, overseen by a strict army doctor who was adamant that I keep my extra weight at twenty pounds. As any pregnant woman knows, mostly you are hungry all the time—except when you're nauseated—so not eating is a never-ending battle. I love food.

Mike, Hazel, and some other friends had driven to Wheeling, West Virginia, to the WWVA Wheeling Jamboree to hear the Osborne Brothers, who were playing that Saturday night. We would have been there with them had it not been for the imminent birth, and when Cory was born we announced the big event by phoning in a request to the Jamboree asking that the Osborne Brothers play "Darling Cory" for Alice, Jeremy, and Cory Foster:

Well the first time I seen Darling Cory
She was settin' on the banks of the sea
Had a forty-four round her body
And a banjo on her knee.

Bobby (b. 1931) and Sonny (d. 2021), "The Osborne Brothers," as they were known, were brothers from Eastern Kentucky whose family, like so many others, needed work and migrated to near Dayton, Ohio, in the 1940s. Bobby played mandolin and had a very high, cutting tenor voice, the envy of many a singer, and Sonny played banjo, sang baritone, and was generally the funny guy. Jeremy and I were big Osborne Brothers fans, and when we were attending Antioch College in the 1960s we got them to come and play a concert there (the first-ever bluegrass concert at a college, though Neil Rosenberg recently told me that the very first might have been Flatt & Scruggs at Gardner-Webb College in the 1950s, according to Louise Scruggs and Earl's older brother Horace).

I have a powerful memory of waking up with Jeremy one morning in Washington, DC, where we were working at our Antioch co-op jobs (internships). We would always set the alarm to the local WAMU bluegrass radio station, and that morning it came alive at 6 a.m. with the refrain "Rubeeeeeee, Ruby! Honey are you mad at your man?"—Bobby's powerful, high tenor voice leading out all by its lonesome until the guitar lead-in runs up to the banjo kicking in for a few measures until Bobby finishes out the verse, holding a note until you think he'll keel over. If you've never heard that song by the Osbornes, it'll blow your socks off. It still blows mine off. What a wonderful way to wake up back in 1957!

The word "parenting" was not in anyone's vocabulary back in 1957, and Jeremy and I were flying by the seat of our pants. We were young, clueless, and very inexperienced. We had no idea what we were getting into or what we were doing. Getting pregnant and giving birth was relatively easy, and after three days we left the army hospital with a baby. What could go wrong? I had read Dr. Spock's book *The Common*

Sense Book of Baby and Child Care, and babies sleep a lot—it'll be a snap! Not having parents or other family around to guide us or help us with raising children (not that we would have listened necessarily), we did a lot of stupid stuff. We prided ourselves on being casual, chill parents. I don't remember thinking very much about safety or germs, and to be honest I don't remember our parent friends running around scrubbing, putting covers on wall sockets and locks on kitchen cabinet doors to keep the kids out either.

I've often analyzed and tried to unpack those times and that lack of concern for the now-obvious pitfalls. Why didn't we ask for help, get babysitters, or organize some kind of support system as people do routinely these days? We didn't have a lot of money, but we weren't exactly poor. I think we saw ourselves as part of the hippie counterculture, "doin' it our way." Our general style was of the loose, laissez-faire, informal, kids-can-sleep-on-the-floor-at-the-party sort—they call it "free range" now, and my grown children have occasionally used this term when reminiscing about their upbringing, although "free range" today strikes me as being nonhovering but at the same time responsible, thought-out, well-taught. Our style back then would most likely be called negligent these days, and honestly, I can't legitimately call it a "style." It was more a stumbling around till it felt right, or until we fell or ran into something—"like a blind hog stumbled on an acorn," as my old fiddler friend Tommy Jarrell used to put it.

I think Jeremy was more emotionally ready to have children. I had some kind of picture of my life that in reality wasn't my truth—I'd be a super mom and we'd have lots of kids and I'd still do whatever I wanted, and somehow we'd live our life happily ever after. As I look back, I think I was way more conflicted about becoming a parent than I ever admitted at the time. And as time passed, doing what I wanted, when I wanted, playing music, living music, was hard for me to reconcile with the daily care of four small children.

I think that my mother, a person who was to some extent thwarted in her aspirations as a musician by severe rheumatoid arthritis, who was "helpless" yet strong and determined, who depended on her husbands to take care of her, yet resisted the very same, set an example of inner conflict that influenced me deeply. Her priority was her illness and the care of herself. Her music lived with her and was necessary, but her children were seldom her priority. And Jeremy clearly had issues too, as I see it, around the fact that his father died in a plane crash in 1945 when Jeremy was ten. He became a "difficult" child, so he was sent away to a boarding school in Massachusetts. He hated it there and wrote letters begging his mother to bring him home, which she eventually did. In the same way that I did, he acted out his grief and anger and made life difficult for his mother and sister. So there we were, stumbling around into adulthood and parenthood.

We returned to Antioch College in 1960 so that Jeremy could get a degree in math. I was pregnant with Jenny, our second child, and I don't remember that it even occurred to me to also try and get my degree—I don't think I really cared. I was certainly not thinking that anything might happen that would necessitate my making a living! And no adults tried to steer me toward a career. It was the 1950s and shows like *Father Knows Best* and *Leave It to Beaver* were the examples of married life and womanhood within it. It was the social order of the day, and although I feel as though in many ways I was unconsciously rebelling against that order, it didn't translate into career action. I audited a couple of classes for a semester: music and German. I really liked the music teacher, Walter Anderson, and I did manage to compose a short piece for piano, but formal music training wasn't my cup of tea; I could never really grasp, or felt the need to grasp, music theory. My childhood piano lessons with Miss Irons and her monthly "teas," where her students played music theory games to win small prizes, were always humiliating in that I was *always* the loser.

I think that one huge reason I was so attracted to traditional music was the informal, nonacademic factor. You didn't have to read notes and if you had a good ear you could learn the music just by listening, watching, and doing. My friend Irene Herrmann (Jeanie McLerie, Irene, and I played together and toured during the late 1970s into the '80s as the Harmony Sisters) told me of her traditional music awakening. She is a classically trained cellist and pianist, and with a few of her classical music friends would occasionally set up on the corner of a downtown San Francisco street to play their string quartets and trios—music stands, sheet music with clothespins, chairs, a whole sidewalk string section—hoping to make a few bucks busking. Then, one day when she was downtown, Irene passed a small string band—Dr. Humbead's New Tranquility String Band—one of the first Bay Area "revival" old-time string bands. They were standing together, playing fiddles, banjo, and guitar; heads bobbing, feet tapping, bodies loose, looking at one another and the crowd, interacting, joking, talking, having a good time. No music stands or sheet music attached with clothespins. Irene said, "I want that!" and thus began her journey into the traditional music world.

There was a lot of interest at Antioch in folk music during the 1950s; people were playing guitars and singing folk songs, and I taught myself to play some rudimentary guitar and banjo, and would haunt the music library for recordings of traditional musicians. When we went back in the early 1960s interest had grown and had moved a bit from "folkie" music to more "authentic" sounds.

In those days Jeremy and I lived and breathed music. Our tiny Yellow Springs apartment quickly became a hub for wonderful gatherings of music, talk, and many poker games. Even though I wasn't a student and was not working a regular job, I didn't feel as though I needed to "keep house," hence dishes went unwashed, house cleaning was at a bare minimum—I wanted to play music. And, by the way I don't remember Jeremy doing that stuff either. He was a wonderful dad—not so good at keeping house.

We discovered that one of the janitors at Antioch played clawhammer banjo, and a local fiddler, Peewee Myers, told us about an event or contest near Dayton called "Kentucky Days," sponsored by the Miami Valley Kentucky Association. A fellow Antiochian from those days, DeeDee Halleck, now a respected media activist and filmmaker,

Jeremy and I are in our Yellow Springs kitchen where most of our life took place: music, poker games, but little housework, ca. 1960. Photographer unknown; courtesy Alice Gerrard.

recently found an old letter she had written to her boyfriend mentioning the contest: "Alice, after hours of persuasion, entered the banjo contest and WON. She is now the Miami Valley Kentucky Association Banjo Champion [I should add that to my résumé]. And she got $5. She had only one competitor but he was damn good. Jerry [Jeremy] says a hell of a lot better than Alice, and I guess he's right but she sure swayed the crowd (it was judged by applause) . . . plus the fact that Cory kept yelling '*Mommy!*' during the whole thing."

Jeremy and I formed a little band, the Greene County Stump Jumpers, and we bonded with another group of musician-students from nearby Oberlin College, the Plum Creek Boys, who had caught the bluegrass music bug in much the same way we had. This band included banjo player Neil Rosenberg, who became professor emeritus in folklore at Memorial University in Newfoundland (now retired), and author of several important books on bluegrass music history. He also wrote the liner notes for the very first Hazel & Alice recording in 1967.

Mayne Smith, one of the small group of Oberlin College bluegrass newbies and a friend of Neil's, remembered his trip to Antioch in 1959 to visit the like-minded bluegrass newbies there who were mainly me and Jeremy. Neil asked Mayne, in his article for *The Bluegrass Situation* (February 10, 2021), what his memories were of this visit:

> At some point, in an afternoon I think, Jeremy put on a tape of the Stanley Brothers in live performance—my gut tells me it was one of the ones Mike Seeger had recorded at New River Ranch in like 1957. As soon as I heard that totally live, undoctored sound I was captivated, and I believe I sat and lay on that hard floor listening to live Stanley Brothers shows (several sets, at least) for hours. My mind was blown. Knowing it was totally live and without studio gimmicks and buried background effects, it came home to me how the fluctuating balance of instruments and voices was accomplished by movement in relation to the microphone and each other, how at times there were lovely breathing spaces in the sound while people shifted from instrumental breaks to solo vocals to harmony vocals. How nobody was using a lot of physical effort to project the sound, yet it penetrated, flowed, darted ahead, waxed and waned like the mating dance of a single complex organism—and how comfortable and familiar the musicians were with what they were singing and playing. I was learning not only about how bluegrass fits together, but also about what a band can be like when it's been playing constantly together, day in and day out, for weeks—for years.

Mayne's response I think perfectly captures what was captivating to so many of us at that time. We were so consumed with enthusiasm for the music that we wanted others to discover and love it too. In early 1960 Jeremy convinced the Antioch student government to let us organize a concert of bluegrass music with the Osborne Brothers.

The plan for the Osborne Brothers concert at Antioch was that Oberlin's Plum Creek Boys and Antioch's Greene County Stump Jumpers (us) would open for them. Years later, Bobby and Sonny Osborne reminisced with me about that concert, remembering how hard they had tried to connect with the strange college audience and how hard it was for the Antioch students to connect with them and this unfamiliar music and stage patter.

In 1973, budding journalist and bluegrass music enthusiast Tom Teepen, who had attended that first concert, wrote in a very funny and painfully detailed article in *Muleskinner News* ("How Many Here Like Baseball?") about the culture shock between the students and the country musicians: "[The Osborne Brothers] didn't know what to expect . . . the audience, primarily of Antioch students, shared their discomfort. . . . The concert started shakily. . . . [The Osborne Brothers] peppered their performance with jokes that usually went over well enough elsewhere but from the college audience won an uncomprehending, stony silence or restless scuffling. . . . [The Osborne Brothers] were visibly growing desperate, and when Bobby tried a between-numbers yarn that began with "How many of you here like baseball?" not a hand went up. "I guess you all don't go much for baseball here," Sonny said, and drew emphatic applause. . . . They both realized that the concert . . . was hanging from the brink. It could take a painful fall into the cultural gap." However, during intermission we made some suggestions as to what folk-tinged material might make more of a connection, and as Teepen wrote, "The second half of the concert was rich with traditional songs: Salty Dog, Pretty Polly, Down In the Willow Garden, Cripple Creek, Wildwood Flower . . . and by 'Cripple Creek' the music had taken fire in the audience. . . . A music and an audience that had been unknown to one another a couple of hours earlier had made some lasting impressions and some lasting friends." It would be a few years before bluegrass became familiar to other college audiences, and before the year was out, the Stanley Brothers and the Country Gentlemen would play there also to audiences that attended, not because they *didn't* know what bluegrass was but because they *did*." And indeed, the following year we brought in the Stanley Brothers for a very successful concert. Teepen, a widely respected journalist with the *Atlanta Journal Constitution*, died in 2017.

Jeremy graduated from Antioch in 1961 and we moved back to Washington, DC, where we had our two boys, Joel and Jesse. There was a quick detour when Jeremy got a job in Virginia Beach, where we enjoyed living, especially because of the beach. Still, we always felt like the DC area was where we wanted to make our home; Virginia Beach was a detour you might say, so when Jeremy found work near DC, we moved back, and were preparing for life with our kids, our music, his job, our friends. We made a down payment on a house in Arlington, Virginia, staying with my cousin in Manassas until the house was settled, and entered Cory in kindergarten. Then early one morning about an hour after Jeremy left for work and I was feeding the kids, I got a phone call from our good friend Tom Morgan, who was at the hospital where the police had taken Jeremy after the car he was riding in was hit head-on by another car. He was dead, killed in a crash, a passenger in a car on the way to work. The doctors had found something in Jeremy's pocket with Tom's phone number on it and I got the call no one ever wants to get. The bottom dropped out, life was upended, and nothing was the same.

A lot of my memories and time frames around the time of Jeremy's death are confused in my mind, and fragmented. Going to court with the children (a lawyer's move so that hopefully they'd give me the maximum allowed in Virginia at that time, $35,000) sticks in my mind. There was grief then, and grief now when my son tells me, "Never a day goes by when I don't wonder what life would have been like if Dad hadn't been killed."

And I sometimes wonder that too, but not every day. Honestly, we were only married for seven years when he was killed. I'm ninety now. Those seven years are a blip on my timeline, but a blip that produced four great children, and in many ways started me on my life in music.

GETTING ON WITH IT

One of the places that soothed my soul was the old 1800s Waterford house in Loudoun County, Virginia where Jeremy had grown up. Jeremy's mother, Beatrice Michelson Foster, kept the family home after her husband (Jeremy's father, Festus) was killed in a plane crash. Waterford was a beautiful little town originally settled by Quakers in about 1733. The place became a kind of refuge for us and others of our friends (and relatives) who were traveling, temporarily homeless, or just visiting. We burned wood in the many fireplaces, cooked, played cards and other games, had endless conversations, played music, smoked cigarettes, and lived a communal life of sorts. After Jeremy died, the children and I, and often friends, would spend weekends there in the beautiful old house with its large yard, outbuildings, and kind neighbors who had known Jeremy all his life. The children, especially, had wonderful times there, and I took loads of photos of them.

Tragically, the back part of the house, where the kitchen with its huge fireplace and dining room lived, burned down in 1968. We went out to visit the damage with my friend Mary Morgan and her children, and of course our dog Ginger. Eventually the house was sold, but I keep it in my heart.

Back to 1964, here I was, a college dropout with four kids between the ages of one and seven, who suddenly had no father. I'd always been fairly independent, but I was not organized, not a planner, and had no sights set on a goal, with one foot in front of the other heading toward that goal. It was kind of like when I was a teenager in Mallorca thinking I'd fall in love and live out the rest of my life there in the sunshine with my trolley conductor boyfriend. How? Why? Well, I never thought about that part. I marvel at my children and grandchildren, who, for the most part, know what they want and set about getting there.

I was able to get the Arlington house down payment back, and I bought a house in Northwest DC with that and the legal settlement, so we had a place to live, and it was our home from 1964 to 1970.

Will Foshag, or Willie, as we knew him (1928–2017), was a quirky, sweet, idiosyncratic genius, a preservationist and aeronautical engineer who specialized in hovercraft development and loved music. A kind and good friend, he was a great comfort to all of us after Jeremy's death. Here he is in the mid-1960s with Jesse (*left*) and Joel in back, cousin Roger in front, and Jenny behind Roger.

I got lots of support during this time. Friends helped me get legal stuff in order, made sure I applied for Social Security. Joan Shagan, a friend in the music scene who didn't play music but loved listening (and was eternally interested in what in the world made these musicians tick) was in graduate school at the University of Maryland. She was getting a clinical psychology degree and was looking for a place to live. My cousin-in-law, a contractor, helped me turn the basement of the new house into a minimal apartment; Joan moved in with her dog, a big gray Weimaraner named Jubal, a yellow cat named Geordie, and an addiction to Coke in the small bottles. She paid rent and took a great interest in the children, often keeping an eye on them for me and letting me know if she thought I was doing the wrong thing with their upbringing. Or with anything else for that matter. Being a psychologist in training gave her a certain authority.

Friends were family—friends like Hazel and Joan, Mike and Marge Seeger, Jim Steele, Lamar and Frances Grier, Tom and Mary Morgan, Ralph Rinzler, Willie Foshag, Marilyn and Bruce MacDonald, our wonderful family dog Ginger, and the many others who saw us through this dark time.

Joan Shagan (*center*) with Ralph Stanley (*left*) and George Shuffler, 1961(?). Cory is hanging out on the far right. Photo by Jeremy Foster; courtesy Alice Gerrard.

Jim Steele was always a great comfort to the kids. Here he is comforting Joel, 1966.

Jim Steele had a family cabin in the mountains of rural Shenandoah County, Virginia, and the children and I, and other friends, would often go up there and hang out for several days at a time. The kids and our dog, Ginger, could run wild, play in the streams and woods and soothe our souls with hiking, swimming, talking, evenings around a wood stove, music. . . . If it was summer the kids went around practically naked. When there might be hunters about, we made all the children *and* Ginger wear bright red fabric capes over their shirts and jackets and Ginger's collar. Occasionally there'd be a little excitement like the time Jim's uncle "Yank," who had come up to go rabbit hunting, returned from his hunt, rifle in one hand and the other holding a dead rabbit by the ears, saying, "Look here kids, it's the Easter Bunny—ain't gonna be no more Easter," his big belly laugh belying the tragedy of such a happening. Like I said, "parenting" wasn't a thing back then.

I was interested in "taking pictures," and took many around there with Jeremy's old camera. Wish I had one of Yank and the Easter Bunny. I drove around the countryside some, visiting the Meems Bottom covered bridge, and wandering around the old cemetery, fascinated by all the old gravestones, imagining the lives and deaths of those long gone.

During the years in DC after Jeremy's death (1964–70), I began to develop my interest in photography. I had Jeremy's old camera, took a class at the Smithsonian, and palled around with my friend Betsy Siggins, a free spirit, idea person, and go-getter, who was also interested in photography and filmmaking. We would dress our kids up and pose them for Christmas card photos, we'd wander around DC and take photos of anything we thought was interesting. I often used my kids as subjects, experimenting with natural and artificial light and the like; they weren't always happy to get on this train with me, but in general they were good sports about it.

Music and photography were healing for me. I eventually bought a Federal enlarger that I hauled around with me for years using it until 1989 or '90. I was more interested in printing than in developing film, so I became friends with the good folks at Asman Custom Photo in downtown DC, who developed my film for me very cheaply and I just printed. I never had a studio or even a space devoted to printing photos.

ABOVE Adventures at Jim Steele's cabin near Mount Jackson in the Shenandoah Valley of Virginia, a place that helped us all to heal. Pictured are (*left to right*) Jeremy Seeger, Jenny Foster, Arley (Chris) Seeger, and either Jesse or Joel Foster.

FACING Me in the late '60s(?). Photographer unknown. I made the sweater, by the way. Courtesy Alice Gerrard.

It was always makeshift—mostly various bathrooms. I loved experimenting with different kinds of paper, watching the pictures gradually appear in the developer, messing with darkening and lightening areas of the photo (photoshopping the old-time way), hanging them to dry . . . and then the great satisfaction of spreading them out on a table—finished.

One of my greatest challenges and always the biggest question after Jeremy's death was, "Who's going to take care of the kids?" Finding a babysitter for a day, a night, a weekend, a week or two . . . it was the constant backdrop to my life. I could take them with me to a party or other event, to a music park, or a friend's house. But the truth was, I didn't know how to live the kind of life (and really didn't want to) where you looked into hiring regular help, or someone to live in the house and help take care of the children, so that you could then set out on your path. Plus, it was not affordable. They were all in school, and some kind of barter would have been hard with four children. At any rate, like so many other single mothers, I cobbled life together as best

FACING Backstage with the Byrds, Nashville, 1968. Clarence White is at center.

ABOVE Merle Haggard at a park show, Culpeper, Virginia, 1969.

it could be cobbled. Sometimes the neighbor kid babysat, sometimes others whose names I can't even remember. Joan lived in the basement and babysat sometimes, but she was in school and was often going to the same events I was going to. It was not an organized life, but I think of those years after 1964, after grief subsided, as years of discovery, excitement, fun, and some chaos.

The music scene was exciting in and around DC in the mid-1960s. *Bluegrass Unlimited*, the first magazine dedicated to bluegrass music, was getting off the ground under the auspices of Pete and Marian Kuykendall. In 1966, the first mimeographed issue came out on 8 × 17-inch paper. The venues were plenty too: the Shamrock, the Red Fox Inn, Ontario Place, Blues Alley, the Cellar Door, and others, were hosts to bluegrass bands and blues, jazz, and folk musicians; the Washington Folklore Society was in full bloom, hosting concerts, workshops, and campout weekends, providing a haven for countless budding and established singers and players. I listened to Skip James at Ontario Place, I listened to the Diz Disley trio with Stéphane Grappelli, and Joe Venuti at a small club on Connecticut Avenue whose name I've forgotten.

ABOVE Ralph Rinzler playing the piano in my living room in Washington, DC, ca. 1968.

FACING Smithsonian Folklife Festival, 1969. Charlie Monroe (guitar), Ralph Rinzler (mandolin). Unknown boy dancing.

I saw Ian & Sylvia at the Cellar Door. And all around DC in Virginia and Maryland were the country music parks and the small, out-of-the-way bars where you could hear the Stoneman Family, Buzz Busby, Red Allen and Frank Wakefield, Benny and Vallie Cain, and countless others.

Local radio station WAMU was going strong with Lee Michael Demsey, Ray Davis, and Dick Spottswood broadcasting bluegrass. John Dildine had a weekly folk music show on WASH-FM. WHAT played country music for a while, and there was WOL-AM with Bob "Nighthawk" Terry.

My old friend Ralph Rinzler (mandolin player, manager and friend of Bill Monroe and Doc Watson, general mover and shaker, and wonderful, energetic, imaginative genius) had moved to town, having been hired by the Smithsonian to work with Jim Morris to develop a folklife festival that became the Smithsonian Festival of American Folklife. Ralph also conspired with bluegrass music promoter Carlton Haney to produce the first weekend-long bluegrass festival in Fincastle, Virginia, in 1965.

Ralph stayed with me for a while until he found a place to live in the Capitol Hill area. He would occasionally take me with him when he went scouting for the Smithsonian Festival—more opportunities to take photos. My children loved him. He'd give them shoulder rides, take them to fun places, give them treats, listen to them, comfort them, all things they really missed with their dad gone.

Labor historian, carpenter, union organizer, shipwright, and professor of folklore and English, the endlessly enthusiastic and lovable Archie Green (d. 2009) was living in town, working with the AFL-CIO and the Smithsonian. While he was there he worked and lobbied tirelessly to win (successfully in 1976) congressional support for the American Folklife Preservation Act that essentially created the American Folklife Center in the Library of Congress. And I kept on taking photographs.

TOP Me taking photos at the Smithsonian Folklife Festival, 1969. (*Standing, left to right*) Fred Price, Clint Howard, Red Parham, Clint's son Clarence, and Fred's son Kenneth. Photographer unknown.

BOTTOM A jam session in my living room in Washington, DC, ca. 1968. (*Left to right*) Ralph Rinzler on piano, Kenny Baker on fiddle, Mike Seeger on banjo, Hazel, and unidentified.

Bill Monroe's extraordinary fiddler Kenny Baker would visit from time to time and try to show me a few licks on the fiddle; Ralph Stanley was playing in town, didn't have a bass, and sent one of the band (I think Jack Cook) to climb in the unlocked window of my locked house and get my bass and bring it to the gig; our faithful dog Ginger wasn't really a watchdog luckily. These were amazing times of discovery.

And what were my children doing through these times? How were they coping? Our old friend Mike Seeger had started coming around. He and Marge had separated; he was renting a place in DC and was on tour a lot. Mike was sad and conflicted over the breakup of his family. He and Marge had three small boys the same ages as my three youngest. I'd known and become friends with Mike through Jeremy in the 1950s, and Marge was a close friend of Jeremy's and mine since our Antioch days. It was Jeremy's suggestion that prompted the meetup that led to her marriage with Mike. So relationships were nothing if not complicated. When her boys were babies and Mike was on tour she often visited Jeremy and me. She remains one of my closest friends today. We often delve into the confluence of circumstances good and bad (always complicated) and relationships that brought us all together and ultimately became our wonderful extended family.

But back in the late 1960s it became clear that their marriage was not going to survive. Mike and I began our relationship at that time with everything very unsettled and unclear; problematic, knotty, peppered with both difficult and good times. He would often bring his children around when they were visiting and we'd do fun things together. I took a batch of photos in 1966 when Mike was in town, visiting and bringing his kids to visit so he could spend time with them during his separation from Marge. I remember the fun we had with all seven of our kids at the old Kennedy Street playground and the zoo. A *Washington Post* article in September 2016 put it this way: It was a great playground until "of course, adult knuckleheads had to mess things up . . . building a wonderful playground but not figuring out how to maintain, adequately staff and keep it running. By the mid to late 70s it was pretty well done, with most of the fun stuff removed."

In 1970 I sold the house in Washington, DC, and Mike and I and my kids moved to Southern Pennsylvania, not far from where Mike's New Lost City Ramblers' bandmate, Tracy Schwarz, had a farm outside of Glen Rock. We bought a beautiful old stone farmhouse with about eighty acres along a small road in a kind of hollow. Hazel's father, Hillary N. Dickens, married Mike and me there on the farm (John Cohen took some nice photos of the wedding), and we settled into rural life with our dog, a lamb, a baby goat, two geese, and several cats. During the summers and many holidays Mike's three boys, Kim, Arley, and Jeremy, would come and stay with us, so there were seven children between the ages of seven and fourteen. A *lot* of great kids.

"WE WEREN'T FARMERS"

—MY SON JESSE, AGE TEN.

"GOOD STUFF, BAD STUFF"

—JENNY, JOEL, AND JESSE

Our "adventure" on the farm was a combination of a lot of fun and a lot of turmoil. Mike was on tour a lot with the New Lost City Ramblers or by himself, and he and I had started doing some touring together during that time as well. If you think finding babysitters back in DC was a problem, try to find ones who are willing to live in the country for two to three weeks. I would get recommendations from friends and sometimes it worked out well, and sometimes not so much. Dale Appleman, an artist friend from DC, recommended her friend Helen Whiting (later cofounder and co-owner of the Regulator Book Store here in Durham on Ninth Street [d. 1999]). Helen was a good caretaker, and being a person who loved to read, as did the kids, they got along fine. There was another young woman the kids really liked who happened to be a graduate of the Cordon Bleu academy in Paris. I got a postcard from her one time when we were in Japan that said, "Jesse eats like a bird: three times his weight in food a day." Another of their favorites was a young woman at loose ends who was a sweet person and an obsessive fan of the Incredible String Band, sometimes described as a Scottish psychedelic folk band. She turned the kids on to the ISB and also to occasional weed, and the list goes on . . .

Although never discussed, it was my unwritten responsibility—my job since they were my kids, not Mike's—to find babysitters. I recently found something that I had put together: directions for babysitters. Aside from the usual list of phone numbers to call, when the trash is picked up, where the ironing board is, how to use the Ashley woodstove, how to clean the Corning stovetop, etc., etc., the seven or so pages read in part:

TOP All seven kids, ca. 1969. (*Standing, left to right*) Arley (Chris) Seeger, Kim Seeger, Jesse Foster, Cory Foster, Jenny Foster; (*sitting at center*) Jeremy Seeger; and (*front*) Joel.

BOTTOM The kids loved the Incredible String Band, as did their babysitter, Sher. The drawing is by Jenny Foster.

Kids are supposed to keep the front porch supplied with wood. However, if any of them are using the axe only one at a time should use it. If Joel is using it, Jesse should be a mile away and vice versa. . . .

The school bus comes around 7:20 and the kids usually get themselves off without me although I try and stumble down once in a while to see them off. . . .

The van is a mess. I meant to clean it out but didn't have time. If the back end sounds like it's falling out it isn't. It's the positraction [when equal power goes to both rear drive wheels] acting up and it has almost since we got the car . . . occasionally it tends to lunge as you go around a curve . . . the windows on the side are taped because they'll fall out (they already have, twice). . . . There is more silver [duct] tape in the kitchen if it looks like they need more tape. . . .

I found another note that was a list written in 1969 by the kids: "Good Stuff, Bad Stuff," about me. There was *nothing* listed on the Good Stuff side, but among the complaints on the Bad Stuff side were sleeping late, paying too much attention to Jesse, "she talks too much on the phone," and she "goes away too much."

When Mike's children came during the summers and some holidays, there were seven kids and generally an "us against them [parents]" mentality, which could be a lot of fun in its own way. I'd say that in general they had a fun time being together, getting into trouble, going to triple-feature horror movies at the drive-in theater, riding down the hill on the zipline, presenting plays in the little outbuilding up the hill. "Pennsylvania Vampire (cheaper than the Broadway production)" was one.

But there were plenty of times I felt overrun by kids, by lack of solitude, and guilt at not quite living up to my image of a strong mother with many children living easily on a farm. Although I made homemade granola and made butter from local cream it wasn't really my thing. Hazel and I were still playing together and doing the occasional gig, but it was made much more difficult because she lived about three hours away and didn't drive. My song "Mama's Gonna Stay" is about such moments:

In the early morning light
I creep on down the stairs
Hush you floor, keep your squeakin' down
And the smell of good hot coffee, and the silence all around

Nothing but my thoughts and the stirring of a song
To break the sad, sweet feeling, lord
Of being all alone. . . .

My cousin Cora Lee and three of her four children moved from California back east after her divorce and bought a farm about five miles from us in Pennsylvania. When Mike was away on tour I remember lots of crazy, fun times with the cousins . . . piling kids into the van and going to drive-in movies, swimming in creeks, going to local country fairs, having big meals together. . . . At the same time, there was a lot of chauffeuring kids around (no public transportation), and when Mike and I started doing some gigs together, there was the continuing babysitting problem, which was left to me to deal with. Practicing with Hazel was problematic. Occasionally she would take a bus up to Pennsylvania to rehearse or I would drive down to DC, but it wasn't easy. In the late 1970s I instigated an unpopular (to everyone else) move back to the DC area and we settled in Garrett Park, Maryland.

THE STRANGE CREEK SINGERS ABROAD

During the late 1960s and early '70s Mike had the idea (he was a good idea man) to form the Strange Creek Singers, a sort of adjunct group alongside Hazel & Alice and the New Lost City Ramblers. The Strange Creek Singers were Hazel, me, Tracy Schwarz, Lamar Grier, and Mike. We toured occasionally both in the United States and overseas, and made one album for Arhoolie Records that is one of my favorites. One memorable tour overseas in 1976 included a trip to Swansea, Wales, to play and sing for coal miners in the Onllwyn Miners Hall.

I found a kind of diary that I typed up during that time: "The place filled up, [they] drank and listened to us and they also sang for us . . . in Welsh. . . . After the program was over we all sang 'Amazing Grace' together in Welsh and English. . . . Then one song led to another—people just didn't want to stop singing . . . the Rose and Crown choir sang for us. . . . It ended with the Welsh National Anthem. . . . After all the singing was done they served us caul, a Welsh soup made up of lamb broth, lamb, carrot and leeks and chunks of bread. And more beer . . ." (There are a couple of clips on YouTube of the Strange Creek Singers at the Miners Hall.)

The event had been organized by Helen Lewis, a Southern radical educator living in Southwest Virginia, whom we got to know through our work with the Southern Folk Cultural Project. Helen was living in Wales at the time working with the coal miners there to build connections between mining communities in Appalachia and Wales. As noted in her 2022 obituary, "Helen taught in colleges and prisons; went to jail for civil rights and stood on picket lines; planted gardens and wrote poetry. In all her work she connected, supported, and pushed people to work together and go a little farther to build communities and make change." That concert and the evening of sharing music in the Onllwyn Miners Hall was wonderful. When Hazel sang her song "Black Lung," it really meant something to the men and women in that room.

From Wales we went on to a music festival in Belfast, Northern Ireland, as my notes reflect: "The first thing we saw in Larne were oil drum barricades around the police station and barricades in front of hotels especially to keep bomb-rigged cars from ramming the building. There was barbed wire everywhere and signs saying 'Lock your car, don't let the bomber get your car' . . . 'Sectarianism kills workers'. . . . Bombed-out pubs dotted the streets and we were often frisked when entering a public space."

WHEELS KEEP TURNING

In the mid-1970s I formed the Harmony Sisters. The impetus for the group was a West Coast tour that our friend John Ullman was putting together. It was to be all women: Ola Belle Reed, myself, and others. I had agreed to do the tour, but I've never enjoyed being onstage, just me and my guitar, so I decided to put together a band. I wanted to include musicians who were on the same page with me in their relationships to traditional music. I got on the phone with two musician friends, Jeanie McLerie and Irene Herrmann. They came to our home in Maryland and the three of us worked out enough repertoire for a couple of sets.

Then the tour fell through. We had worked hard, put together original and traditional songs with imaginative and wonderful harmonies, and we had *so* much fun, so we thought why waste it all? We decided to take it on the road. We got on the phone, booked gigs, and for several years we did a couple of tours a year, one out West and one in the East, and we made two albums for Flying Fish Records that we later released as one CD (*The Harmony Sisters: The Early Years*). One of our guiding principles was to mainly do music that we had a personal connection to. Hence our Cajun and New Mexican songs and tunes (and an occasional original song or tune) from Jeanie who spent a lot of time with elders Denis McGee, Canray Fontenot, and many others down in Louisiana, and with traditional fiddlers where she currently lived in New Mexico; hence the traditional Italian tunes of Lorenzo Tunzi, an older Italian neighbor of Irene's in California from whom she learned many fine mandolin tunes. I brought original material plus many of the tunes I'd learned from old friends like Luther Davis, Tommy Jarrell, Bertie Mae Dickens, and others.

Both Irene and Jeanie were great cooks and enjoyed making meals, and we put this talent to good use during concerts. Often, instead of killing time with jokes or patter, we'd give out recipes to the audience. One of our favorites was a recipe from Irene's mom that we turned into a song: "Beer Bread," sung in three-part harmony acapella: "Well you take 3 cups of flour and 2 pinches of salt, / 12 ounces of beer so you can taste that malt. . . ."

During this time with the Harmony Sisters my marriage of ten years to Mike started to fall apart, and in 1980 we called it quits. There were lots of reasons—most have been written about in songs from time immemorial, and in several of mine, including "Sad Affairs":

These are sad affairs, such sad affairs
But the saddest affair—
Is that most likely, soon if not sooner
I won't even care. . . .

Other reasons for the split were totally personal to the two of us and our particular personalities, histories, hangups, needs, and unwillingness or inability to accommodate one another, and a big one for me: Mike had an affair. As a friend told someone who was in the middle of a similar situation: "He left his first wife to be with you; what makes you think he wouldn't do the same thing to you?" Mike moved to Staunton, Virginia, and I moved to Nashville to stay for a while with my friend Anne Romaine until I figured out what I was going to do next. Mike's affair didn't work out, he eventually remarried a lovely woman, and they lived a loving and happy life together before he died of cancer in 2009. Before he died, he took on the project of making sure our *Bowling Green* LP would live on in CD format. I recently found an old email from 2008 wherein Mike, ever the perfectionist, was trying to make sure the notes were coming along and checking on details like copyrights and graphics, wanting my opinion on the reference disc: "Let me know what you think. We're real close to the finish line." (*Bowling Green* is available as a download on Bandcamp.)

Mike was very important in my life; an old friend, a huge influence, an adversary, a musical partner. It wasn't always easy, but it was mostly interesting. He was a fine musician, and he cared deeply for the older musicians he learned from and advocated for. He was a good person. Although not an academic himself, he helped shape the course of traditional and revival music within academia as well as in the public sector.

In 1980, I moved to Galax, Virginia, where I spent the next nine years playing with, spending time with, documenting and learning from older traditional musicians. I played in a couple of bands; I lived and breathed old-time music, and I started the *Old-Time Herald* magazine in 1987.

Chapter 2

HAZEL DICKENS

That's for me to know and you to find out.

—Hazel Dickens (when somebody would ask her age)

We used to be a family in our little cabin home
Whose windows they are broken and whose chimney's dark and cold
But jobs were hard to find back then, it wasn't easy to survive
So one by one we all left home to change our way of life. . . .
You gave me a song of a place that I call home
A song of now, a song of then, a song of yet to come.

—"You Gave Me a Song" (words and music by Alice Gerrard)

There are a lot of memories that are pretty foggy, but I remember one in particular, when Jeremy said to me in early 1953, "There is this little skinny girl with a great big voice that you've got to meet." Meet her I did, and we shared a musical partnership for many years.

Hazel Dickens was born in the coal mining area around Mercer County, West Virginia, in 1925, and had moved, gradually, along with much of her family, to Baltimore after World War II. Like many other Southerners, they hoped to find better work and a better life, and Hazel worked as a waitress, and in factories like Continental Can and Dixie Cup. She was shy and very self-conscious, aware of her lack of formal education, her accent, clothing, and many of the cultural differences that set her apart; she told me about the time someone made fun of her for calling Pepsi and Coke "pop" instead of "soda"—just one of a thousand cuts. Country music is full of songs about leaving the country for the city, hard times in the city, not finding a better life there, longing for home, disillusion, and breakup of families. These songs are staples of country music—"Streets of Baltimore" and "Detroit City" are two that come to mind. I wrote on the subject in my song "Sky over Michigan":

I traded quiet country evenings for bright city sounds
Hard work and worry for hard work and doubt
And this dirty old factory job in Detroit town is a far cry
From a glass slipper & a satin ball gown

By coincidence, Hazel met Mike Seeger when he was working at a tuberculosis sanitarium outside of Baltimore, where one of her brothers was a patient. Through Mike she met other people, including Alyse Taubman, a kind-of-lefty bohemian social worker and music lover who took Hazel under her wing, encouraging her to believe in herself. She became a strong mentor and important friend to Hazel. I believe that I first met Hazel at one of many music parties at Alyse's apartment in Baltimore.

Hazel had a wicked sense of humor and a twinkle in her eye.

House music party, Washington, DC, 1962. (*Left to right*) Hazel, me, Rick Churchill. Photo by Jeremy Foster; courtesy Alice Gerrard.

One of our house parties in Washington, DC, 1962. Hazel is sitting under an old flyer for the Carolina Tar Heels. Photo by Jeremy Foster; courtesy Alice Gerrard.

She didn't immediately trust anyone and liked keeping her "business" to herself. Country smart, she'd grown up hard and poor. Her father, H. N. (Hillary) Dickens was a powerful singer and banjo player but gave the banjo up when he joined the Primitive Baptist church in his early twenties. (Later, Mike Seeger recorded Hillary's singing and banjo playing for the album *Old-Time Tunes of the South* on Folkways Records.) Hazel's mother was a quiet, sweet woman, very deferential to her husband, and not a singer or musician that I can remember, although most of Hazel's eleven siblings sang and played. Hazel had a singing voice that could nail you to the wall, the kind of voice that embodied the "high lonesome sound" to me. She played guitar and bass well enough to occasionally fill in with some local bluegrass band at some random bar gig. But it was that voice! Edgy, piercing, high, lonesome, cutting, and raw: Hers was an oasis in the desert of pretty, sweet voices emerging during the folk revival of the late 1950s and early 1960s.

I was in awe of Hazel's singing, trying to grasp hold of its mysterious power for a long time, listening to her, looking to her as a mentor, learning from her. She was older, generally streetwise and street-smart, and in this world of music and bridging cultures, with her innately suspicious and private nature, she knew what was best. We gradually became friends, and when at some point someone at some music party suggested we try singing together, it seemed like a good idea. It was always informal, and we never considered that we might take it further.

Our recording career started with another party, as I remember, where Peter Siegel was present. He was a young music enthusiast from New York who was heavily involved in the New York City folk scene as both musician and engineer during the early 1960s. Both Peter's and my memories are a bit hazy about the circumstances, but between the two of us, we remember that he and his friend David Grisman, both in their late teens, had come down to DC from New York to attend a bluegrass festival that got rained out. Somehow Peter and David ended up at a music party at my cousin's house on the edge of Georgetown. Hazel

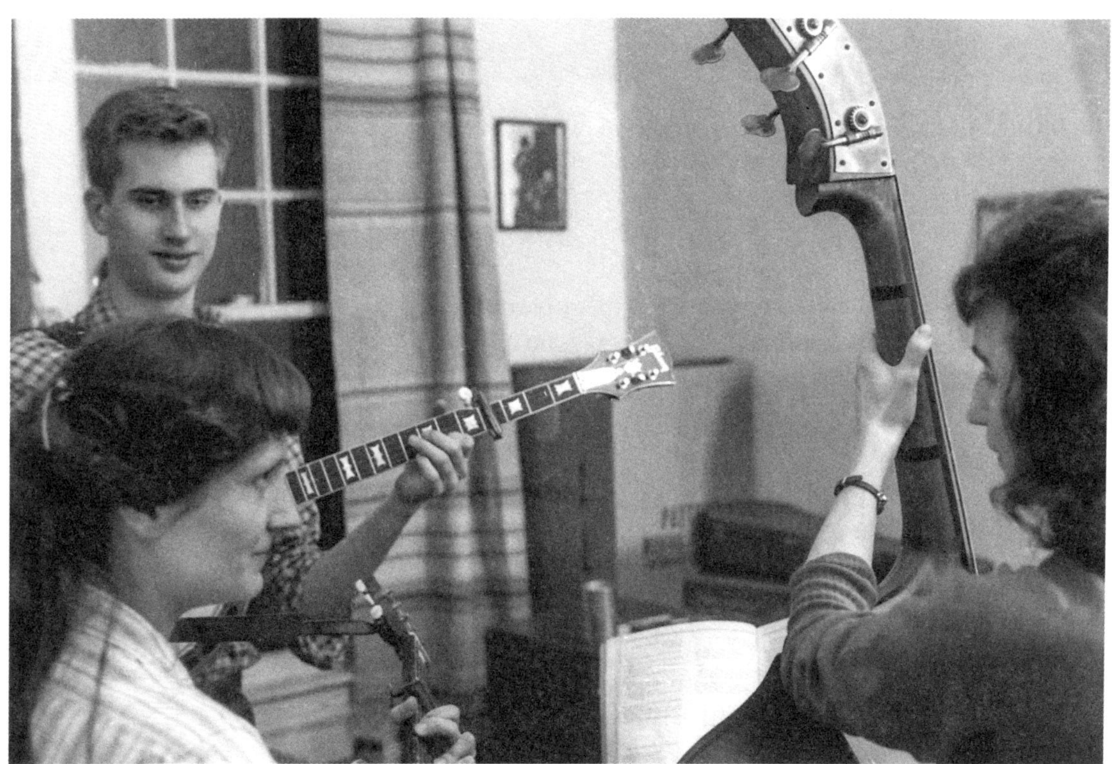

Hazel and me singing at a party at our house in DC, 1962. Rick Churchill is playing the banjo with us. Photo by Jeremy Foster; courtesy Alice Gerrard.

Newport Folk Festival, 1966. Peter Siegel with Hazel. Peter was the recording engineer and producer of our first recording for Folkways Records.

and I were there, and of course we were singing. I checked the notes to *Pioneering Women of Bluegrass*, where both Hazel and I as well as Peter remembered some of the details: "I heard you guys sing in the kitchen and I thought you were great singers and I was totally knocked out." [Peter]. "I remember us sitting on the floor and singing. David and Peter . . . asked if we'd ever thought of recording. . . . David said we'd need to get a tape together and he would speak to Moses 'Moe' Asch, owner of Folkways Records. We [recorded the demo tape] in Pete Kuykendall's basement." [Hazel]. Peter thinks that Mike Seeger, who had recorded several LPs of traditional music for Folkways and had a good business relationship with Moe Asch, also put a good word in for us.

Moe, a Polish immigrant and son of writer Sholem Asch, founded Folkways Records in New York in 1948. The label was known for putting out huge collections of rare, little-known music and spoken-word recordings of all kinds. "He recorded the world" as someone recently noted. Some of these recordings became classics and were revered around the world—Leadbelly, Woody Guthrie, Pete Seeger, Ella Jenkins, and countless others. Others remained known to few or to specialized audiences, but all were available and remain so to this day through Smithsonian Folkways Recordings. Given Moe's wide and varied taste, and perhaps a little prodding from Mike, he agreed to put out a recording of Hazel & Alice. I found a contract that I think is for the first recording of Hazel Dickens and Alice Foster (that was me) dated November 17, 1965. From what I can tell, we were paid $200 with a $75 advance against royalties of 25 cents for each album sold. We were thrilled.

Our first recording! Our good friend Lamar Grier (d. 2019) would play banjo, Hazel the bass, David Grisman the mandolin, and I guitar. All we needed was a fiddler. Robert Russell "Chubby" Wise, a well-known bluegrass fiddler who had played and recorded with Bill Monroe, among others, happened to be living in the DC area at the time, playing at the Famous Bar & Grill across from the Trailways Bus Depot in downtown Washington. Jeremy thought it would be quite a coup if we could get Chubby to play with us on the recording, but we had never met him. Tom Morgan, a close friend and fellow musician who knew him, gave him a call. Tom said, "I have some friends who are trying to cut an album, would you be kind enough to help them out? I like to have dropped my teeth when [Chubby] said, 'Yeah, I'll do it.' He was congenial and supportive."

He was, indeed, chubby, happy, smiling a lot, and all about getting the job done. This was before ProTools. As Peter remembered, "It was one AKG-D24 microphone, a borrowed Nagra III P tape recorder, acetate tape, borrowed speakers [so Peter could play the takes back for us to hear], and mostly one- or two-take songs."

Peter remembers that Moe Asch gave him $75 to make the recording, $37.50 so he could buy tape and a bus ticket, and the other $37.50 when he was finished. "I thought it was big-time," he said. "I bought twelve reels of tape and a bus ticket."

Hazel and I were busy planning the recording, choosing material, and practicing. It was during this time, in September 1964, that Jeremy was killed. Peter remembers wondering whether we'd go through with the recording or not, but we did, probably in early 1965, with a lot of help and support from many friends. We recorded in Pierce Hall, part of the All Souls Unitarian Church at Fourteenth and Harvard Streets in Northwest DC—a hall known by music people for its good acoustics. Hazel remembered that it cost fifty dollars to rent.

Hazel and I recorded a second album for Folkways shortly after the first one, *Won't You Come and Sing for Me*. It wasn't released until 1973, at about the same time that we released our first Rounder Records album. (Apparently Moe had forgotten about it.) My friend Betsy

Promo photos of Hazel and me by Betsy Siggins, a dear friend, Washington, DC, 1969. Courtesy Alice Gerrard.

We were getting bored with promo shots, and Betsy decided we should try some shots for the fun of it. She had tons of props lying around her house—boa, net stockings, peacock feather, and so on—and it became a fun-time cheesecake session. We never used the photos for anything, and a friend stored them in the office of the *Great Speckled Bird* (indie progressive newspaper) in Atlanta, promising he'd keep them on the q.t. Photo by Betsy Siggins; courtesy Alice Gerrard.

Siggins took a number of wonderful photos of Hazel and me at this time, which we used for the cover of *Won't You Come and Sing for Me*. I remember those photo sessions—lots of messing around, indoors and out, trying different backgrounds, lighting, props, outfits. She had cool old furniture in her house, and lots of old pieces of clothing: boas, peacock feathers, net stockings, cigarette holders, and the like that we worked with when we got fed up with playing it straight. Why not mess around? Put three creative women together with a camera and props and watch out!

GETTING NOTICED

The chronology of events is kind of jumbled in my mind due to the trauma of Jeremy's death and the stress of figuring out how to go on. Luckily, as I said, I had many good friends, I had my kids, I had music, and Hazel was always there.

Hazel and I were beginning to try and get a few gigs in a sort of haphazard way. We weren't beating the bushes for work—actively and methodically seeking out music gigs, planning toward a career, or realistically thinking about making a living playing music and touring. Hazel had a nine-to-five job, and I had four kids. But a lot of people liked our music, thought we should get out there, and suggested us for gigs now and then. Bill Monroe hired us to play at Bean Blossom (his bluegrass festival in Indiana), and Mike Seeger and Ralph Rinzler suggested us for the Newport Folk Festival. Hazel was in a romantic relationship with Ken Irwin, the cofounder of Rounder Records, and when we started recording for Rounder he was extremely encouraging, sending gigs our way, urging us to take them. Hazel and I started going on the Southern Folk Cultural Revival Project (SFCRP) tours, often twice a year and usually for a week at a time. I feel as though, in many ways, the tours helped Hazel to find her voice and gave her permission to look inside herself and express her feelings and views, and the radicalism that was a product of years of poverty, injustice, and inequality.

So, things were happening for us. There were some Hazel & Alice gigs that were memorable in those early days. I remember one at the Fairfax Bar and Grill when Bill Monroe showed up and sat in with us. Someone managed to take a picture of us (looks like an old color Polaroid), kind of faded now, that takes prime place in my home to this day. In later years I was interviewing Hazel and she remembered a time in the mid-1960s when we got a gig at the Hawk and Dove, a bar in the Capitol Hill area that was a watering hole for a lot of politicos.

(I'd totally forgotten this, and only vaguely remember now.) Hazel said they asked us to leave after one set, and she didn't remember if they paid us. Apparently, the manager thought our music was a downer for the bar crowd. According to Hazel, she announced to the bar patrons in typical feisty fashion as we packed up, "If you like this music come on to the house [that is, Alice's] and we'll play [there]."

Another memorable gig (well, not so much the gig, but the trip) was when Hazel and I were at one of the Canadian folk festivals and we were flying back to Washington, DC, with Elizabeth Cotten, who had also performed at the festival—accompanying her through customs and on the flight: "Do you have anything to declare, Ms. Cotten?"

"What do you mean?"

"Did you buy anything while you were here in Canada? Any items, any food. . . ."

"Well, all I bought was a little piece of pie and it wasn't any good."

After a bit of a holdup at customs we were running late and afraid we'd miss our flight if we didn't get a move on, so we put Elizabeth in a wheelchair and ran to the gate; missed the flight anyway, and the three of us sat in a bar till the next flight, Hazel and I sipping on cocktails and Elizabeth in her wheelchair sipping on something nonalcoholic. Always an adventure.

PLAYING IN A MAN'S WORLD

A lot of our development as artists was happening during the burgeoning women's liberation movement. Hazel and I were in some ways a bit clueless about the movement back in the 1970s. We were at another Canadian folk festival (I think it was Mariposa outside Toronto). I had recently written "Custom Made Woman Blues," and we were performing in a "women's songs" workshop in the afternoon, where for the first time I decided to sing this newly minted song. The audience gave me a standing ovation, and I had to sing it again. *What was going on?* We also noticed that there were lots of women (sometimes mostly women) at many of our concerts, especially up North. We sensed something was going on but weren't quite sure what it was. Whatever it was, it was welcome, and we felt embraced and supported by the wave that was growing. In one place we played, there were all women, and they didn't allow men at all. That was a bit of a step too far, as far as we were concerned back then, but it's true that often you have to step over the line to even be able to come up to it. And like all movements the groundswell was happening and we felt like it spoke to us as well in our capacities as women trying to play music in a mostly man's world, as a mother trying to balance children and music (not too successfully), encouraging our voices, supporting feelings and realizations about how we could live our lives.

As I mentioned, Hazel was a private person, didn't give her trust lightly, didn't want people to know her business or her age. About the age she was adamant. "That's for me to know, and you to find out" she would say, if she said anything. And she stuck to it like white on rice. None of us knew exactly what her age was. In the mid-1970s, the Strange Creek Singers (Mike, Hazel, me, Lamar Grier, and Tracy Schwarz) were touring in Europe and we crossed many borders going from country to country. Somewhere along the way I was sitting in the front passenger seat and everyone gave me their passports to hand out the window to the border personnel. I took a very quick look at Hazel's—1925. There it was. I never told her I'd found out and even after she died many articles listed her birthdate as 1935, which was the date she gave out when she couldn't avoid giving out some date for an interview or some such. She was definitely hardcore to the end.

Another Betsy Siggins photo taken in her basement in 1969, before we couldn't sit on the ground like that anymore.

After we unwrapped a gift from Hazel, I kept the wrapping paper that she had modified to reflect her feelings. (I don't remember what the gift was.)

When Hazel and her husband Joe Cohen split up in 1968, she left Baltimore, got a job at a Mexican import store, and moved in with the kids and me in DC for a while until she found her own apartment on the outskirts of Georgetown, not far from where she worked. It remained her home for the rest of her life.

We practiced a lot while she was living with us, often recording what we were doing on reel-to-reel tape so that we could listen back. It was a good way to hear what was working and what wasn't; I stumbled on some of these practice tapes in my closet some fifty years later and used material from them for the *Sing Me Back Home* project released in 2018 on Free Dirt Recordings. As I listened to these old tapes from the 1960s, I was amazed at how good we sounded, and how imaginative we were in trying new material and arrangements. It was pretty cool. Sometimes I heard kids crying or fussing in the background, trying to get our attention. There were many of these practice sessions, almost always against the sounds of small children needing something, and "dishes to wash and a house to clean," as Bill Monroe sang in his "True Life Blues." (Housework was always low on my priority list.) I remember one session in the kitchen of our Washington, DC, row house with my young daughter, Jenny, sitting in an overstuffed chair in her nightgown, cross-legged, fingers stuffed in her ears, as Hazel and I wailed away, oblivious.

Bill Monroe

Bill Monroe (the "grandfather of bluegrass") was a big presence in our lives. Our relationship with him was perhaps unusual in that we, as women, maintained a friendship with him that was completely platonic. We loved and respected his music and in turn I think he felt much the same. Despite his reputation as a womanizer, that aspect of his life never spilled over into his relationship with us; he liked us and took a personal interest in our music, liked our singing, and wanted to help us when he could. He was also close to my friend Joan Shagan, who lived in the basement apartment. She, as a psychologist in training, was always fascinated by what made musicians tick, and Bill was endlessly fascinating to her. Often, if he was playing in the area he'd stop by with the band, park his big bus in front of the house (much to the chagrin of neighbors, I'm sure, although nobody complained), and we'd visit, play music, do some eating, and he'd hand out quarters to the kids (they adored him of course). It was on one of his stopovers that Bill suggested Hazel and I learn his beautiful, heartbreaking song "The One I Love Is Gone." I remember the moment in my living room by the fireplace, Bill turning to say, "I think this would be a good song for you and Hazel," and proceeding to teach it to us. Another time he counseled us, "If you need to sing a song in G# or F# (which we often did) and the band can't play it in that key, fire you that band and get you another one!" I remember that like it was yesterday, and these days I often pass Bill's advice on to singing students. I sometimes interviewed him for various recording projects and articles I was working on and talked with him a lot one on one. He always reached back into deep feelings to express how he felt about music, about his childhood, and I felt privileged that he shared those feelings with me.

Bill Monroe having fun with my son Joel at the Warrenton, Virginia, bluegrass festival, 1966.

CHANGES

As Hazel and I worked more, I was beginning to feel like I needed a change of some kind. A lot of the people who influenced me as I was diving into music were multitaskers in a sense—people like Jeremy, Mike, Ralph, Anne Romaine, John Cohen—who played the music, but also advocated for, wrote about, and photographed it—variations on "Don't give up your day job." Or maybe because there was much to love around the music I felt a need to explore some of those aspects. I wasn't sure what or how; it was just a feeling that fed on some other issues in our relationship. It seemed to me that Hazel and I were hanging on to our old roles instead of growing in relationship to one another, roles that were comfortable, but not realistic.

In addition, several ongoing issues were nagging me. The two of us were often singing outside of our comfort zones—Hazel higher than comfortable and me lower. Hazel had a voice and a soulfulness that transcended, in many ways, her tendency to often sing off pitch. I finally decided to talk with her about it, wondering if there was someone she'd trust to work with her on this issue. We both thought that Ethel Raim, a powerful singer and leader of the Pennywhistlers Balkan singers, would be a good choice. (Ethel also wrote some of the liner notes to our second Rounder album.) Hazel liked Ethel and agreed to get in touch with her but never did. I had the sense that her feelings might have been hurt by my bringing up the subject. Nobody had ever talked with her about pitch issues before, although many people she worked with were aware of the problem. I think she was aware there was a problem but didn't quite know what it was, and nobody had ever sought to disturb those waters.

We were in the process of recording the second Rounder album and it was taking a very long time, lots of redos, often due to those pitch issues, plus an incident during this session that was kind of a final straw for me. I had written a song, "Beaufort County Jail," about the 1975 Joan Little case in North Carolina where Joan, a Black woman, was raped by her jailer, and she stabbed him to death with an ice pick that he'd brought into the cell.

Hot summer night in the Beaufort County jail
Hmmmm
Locked her up, jailer kept the key
He did, he kept the key.
Black woman in a white man's jail

No one to call a friend
Jailer watched that woman by day and night
No mercy in a white man's jail

I remember that Ken Irwin had some hesitation about including it on the LP. I remember fighting very hard for the song—it finally was included—but during all of it Hazel didn't back me up. I felt abandoned by both Ken and Hazel. Ken was in a romantic relationship with Hazel, which definitely complicated everything, and I've often wondered if, in spite of our long and close friendship, there was something that made her harbor some mistrust or caution around the differences in our backgrounds and how we grew up. And maybe she had similar feelings around my relationship to Mike that I had with her and Ken. I'll never know. But all of it fed into my need to do something else, and in 1976, I ended our music partnership. Years later, Ken Irwin reminded me (I guess I had blocked it out) that the Rounder folks made a trip to Washington, DC, to try and talk me out of quitting.

It was very hard for both of us. Hazel felt betrayed, and for many years afterward we didn't see much of one another. I felt especially bad for my kids, because she was basically "Aunt" Hazel to them all, and she suddenly disappeared from their lives. This was the subtext for my song "Life's Other Side Comin' Down":

Oh it's hard to admit what we've known for so long
That goin's good as gone, and what goes comes on round
And life's other side is comin' on round
Gotta jump or I'll drown.

Hazel went on to wonderful things; she had total support from Rounder Records, she was writing great songs, becoming more active in political issues, mostly surrounding coal and miner's rights—issues very dear to her as she grew up surrounded by the devastation that mining caused, both environmental and physical. And she understood the people and the culture of coal. She received many accolades throughout her life, including the National Endowment for the Arts (NEA) Heritage Fellowship.

We reunited in 1997 after banjoist and scholar Bill Evans suggested a Hazel & Alice reunion tour to Randy Pitts, a mover and shaker who was a booking agent for the Freight and Salvage Coffeehouse in Berkeley, California. Randy, after talking with each of us, persuaded us to do a limited tour. With the Strawberry Festival near Yosemite National Park as the linchpin gig, we also did *A Prairie Home Companion* and gigs in Seattle; Vancouver, British Columbia; Berkeley; Davis; and other cities. The tour was very successful, and we mostly had fun; lots of folks came out to see and hear us; we had a great band—Jody Stecher, Brantley Kearns, and Todd Phillips—to back us up.

After that tour, Hazel and I didn't have any illusions that we would pick up professionally where we left off in 1976; much had changed and we were happy doing our own things, but we enjoyed being together and occasionally doing gigs together. She joined the family for Thanksgiving every year, or if my kids weren't in town we might go out to a favorite restaurant for Christmas dinner. We never spoke again about the breakup or what led to it, and that seemed the right thing to do. It was swept under the rug, and it didn't really matter. It was during this time that together we wrote a second verse to "The One I Love Is Gone" (Bill Monroe had only written one verse and the chorus). We never recorded the new verse, but I include it these days whenever I sing the song:

I don't know, I don't know
What I'll do without your love
How my heart can ever live with all this pain;
So I'll wander all my life
Like a lonely homeless dove
Alone, with no one to love.

Hazel's reluctance to let people "know her business" took on a whole new meaning when she told me about her stroke. It happened during a Saturday night (I don't remember the date, but sometime around 2008) when she was in bed. She woke up and discovered that basically she couldn't move; couldn't get out of the bed. The telephone was in the living room—she didn't have a cell phone. So she lay there and eventually, through sheer willpower was gradually able to roll out of bed and drag herself into the bathroom where she remained for several hours, then dragged herself to the couch near the phone. But instead of phoning 911, she waited until Monday morning, called her doctor, and took a cab to his office. I asked her why she didn't call 911 as soon as she was by the phone, and she said something to the effect of, "I didn't want an ambulance pulling up with lights and commotion and everyone knowing my business!" As a friend who also knew her remarked, "That's *so* Hazel!"

Sometime later, my son and I were going to visit Hazel; we knocked and knocked and banged on her apartment door—no answer. The apartment was on the ground floor and Jesse walked around trying to look in the windows but couldn't see anything. We were worried about another possible stroke, so we called the super of the building and he came with a key and started unlocking her door. Just as the door was opening, here comes Hazel all pissed off and annoyed that we were causing a commotion possibly heard by the neighbors in the building: "I'm fine," she announced. And she was. Until she wasn't.

I was happy that we had time to be together and "bring back the years" before she died in 2011. And I was honored to walk out with her favorite nephew Arnold "Buddy" Jr. to accept Hazel & Alice's induction into the International Bluegrass Music Association (IBMA) Hall of Fame in 2017.

Hazel was a strong woman who grew up wanting to be somebody, preferably a singer. With music all around her growing up, it was part of her, especially the searing unaccompanied singing of the Primitive Baptist church and the powerful singing of her father, who was a "lay" preacher in the church. When she moved to Baltimore, she found a music home of sorts, singing and playing in the music bars that lived on every corner in areas of the city, providing both comfort and trouble to the many displaced hillbillies. But she was increasingly aware of how women were treated. As she put it, "You were either good enough to be their wife, or bad enough to be their whore. I just wanted to play music." And she did. She put up with a lot of bullshit at first but soon found a community of friends and musicians in Baltimore and Washington, DC, who encouraged and appreciated her, and she became part of that community. But she never lost sight of her family, her roots, and her home, as she expressed in her song "West Virginia My Home":

West Virginia, oh my home.
West Virginia, where I belong.
In the dead of the night, in the still and the quiet
I slip away like a bird in flight
Back to those hills, the place that I call home.

Society doesn't make it easy for women to find their own way. Expectations are still built around a "woman's place." Hazel had lots of "smart-alecky" things to say about that, but one I remember particularly was when we were on the road on a Southern Folk Cultural Revival Project tour traveling through a stretch of roadwork with "Men Working" signs everywhere: "You don't see any of those signs say, 'Women Working,' do you?"

Widen, West Virginia, 1967. While Mike Seeger and I were traveling around in West Virginia we chanced on this old gentleman (William Bragg) sitting on his porch playing the banjo and guitar. Screeching to a halt, we jumped out the car and started talking to him and got around to asking if he was okay with us recording some of his music. He was fine with it and started playing a lot of great tunes. In this photo he is playing one of our guitars. Soon a gaggle of curious local teenage boys gathered and both listened and helped out with the recording. It was a nice afternoon. Mike ended up using one of these photos as the cover to his *Close to Home* recording project.

Chapter 3

FINDING THE FOLK, REACHING FOR THE ROOTS

American traditional music, roots music, or folk music, whatever you want to call it, lives among us. A companion to our everyday lives, it lives in the home with family and friends, in living rooms, churches, on front and back porches, family reunions, Ruritan clubs, bars, juke joints, local fiddlers conventions, fiddlers "picnics," benefits, dances, and more—any excuse to have a little music. And at these places and at these events, I took photos.

Many things have changed since I started taking those photos. Some of the dances have disappeared, many of the country music parks are gone, festivals have gone or changed, new ones take their places, the contexts change—and the music lives on, ever vibrant, as people find new ways to merge their love of the music with the ever-changing world around them.

CHASING THE MUSIC

The alarm rings. It's a sunny summer Sunday morning in Washington, DC, in 1961. A typical weekend morning when we'd go to hear some music, heading up to Sunset Park, the eight country acres owned by the Waltman family in southern Chester County, Pennsylvania, that had served since the 1940s as a venue for traveling country musicians. This week, the Stanley Brothers, Carter and Ralph, are going to be there. Jeremy and I drive to Baltimore to the house on Eager Street to pick up Mike and Alyse, then swing by and pick up Hazel from her apartment before we head up Route 1 to West Grove, Pennsylvania. Alyse and Hazel always made fried chicken, deviled eggs, potato salad, sandwiches, and other picnic delights, which we packed into the car along with tape recorders and instruments. Excitement mounted as we neared the Pennsylvania-Maryland line and entered the domain of brother and sister Alec Campbell and Ola Belle Campbell Reed, Ted Lundy, Deacon Brumfield, and Sonny Miller (the New River Boys and Girls). *Campbell's Corner* on WCOJ, "The Voice of Chester County," broadcast live from a small store in nearby Oxford, Pennsylvania.

Jeremy and Mike would set up their tape recorders and mics, joining other new fans who might be there, among them John Cohen, a young photographer, guitarist, and banjo player from New York City; Jody Stecher, a multi-instrumentalist and singer from Brooklyn; David Grisman, the noted mandolin player from Passaic, New Jersey; and others—all of whom would soak up the sounds and licks, and all of whom would later became renowned for their music, expertise and innovative spirit. In fact, David Grisman was the mandolin player on Hazel & Alice's first two recordings for Folkways Records.

During the ride to New York to record one of those albums, I remember David lying on the floor of the van, trying to help Hazel get on a difficult harmony part for "The One I Love Is Gone." I don't know why he was on the floor; I think he was trying to get her to sing a minor harmony note against a minor chord somewhere in the first line, and she wasn't hearing it. I've noticed that often in traditional music the player or singer will hear a major note against a minor chord or vice versa. Often old-time tunes and songs will have that sound. To me it gives a song more grit and tension—a good thing!

At the music park, Hazel and Alyse would lay claim to one of the old wooden picnic tables and unpack the food. I'd chase the kids around, brush off the dirt, and feed the youngest, hand out small change so

Bill Birchfield, banjo, and his father, Joe Birchfield, fiddle, 1987. The original band, the Roan Mountain Hilltoppers, included Creed, Joe's brother, on banjo, Bill on guitar, and Bill's wife Janice on washtub bass. Bill had a unique way of playing guitar and banjo, fretting with his right hand coming down on top of the strings rather than wrapping around from underneath like most players.

they could play the carnival games or ride the rickety Ferris wheel back in the corner. There was music being played on an outdoor stage, people sitting on benches, and the kids having fun, running free collecting pop bottles and lots of dirt. Someone would be bound to keep an eye open, and they didn't wander too far. The park was in Amish country, and the Amish also came to hear the music. You'd often see them sitting together on the wooden benches, the women and girls in their white *kapps* and plain dark dresses, and the boys and men in their white shirts and dark trousers, savoring the sounds of fiddles and banjos, their horses and buggies parked in a special place away from the cars.

There were lots of outdoor country music parks dotting the landscape, mostly in rural areas, sometimes in a field, sometimes in a wooded grove, sometimes here and gone, hastily put together, sometimes more stable, sometimes lasting for a few years, sometimes many. They were all within a few hours of the Baltimore–Washington, DC, area, within reach of the recently transplanted, mainly white Southerners who had come north to get jobs during the 1940s war years; they were a loyal and enthusiastic audience.

And, increasingly, you'd see the young middle-class folks like me, Jody, Mike, Jeremy, and others who were discovering the music, coming to learn, soak it up, and be part of it all. Country bands played the parks, too—folks like George Jones, the Louvin Brothers, Kitty Wells, Ernest Tubb, and Loretta Lynn—but we were more focused on bluegrass music at that time. And even though most of the players we saw, and *wanted* to see, were men, that doesn't mean that women didn't play a big role in the scene in those days, and they had an outsized influence on me and my musical life.

A jam session at Bill Monroe's Bean Blossom (Indiana) Festival, with Bill Monroe at center, 1969. Note only one woman (with back to camera) in the group.

And although most of the musicians were men, as a young woman it was thrilling for me to see such powerhouses as Wilma Lee Cooper, Ola Belle Reed, Donna, Roni, and Patsy Stoneman. I knew I'd never wear those crinolines like Wilma Lee, but I coveted her right-arm rhythm on that Martin D-45 guitar! I knew I'd never wear go-go boots and dance around while playing the mandolin like Donna Stoneman or be the wry comedienne like her sister, banjo player Roni. But they were playing lead instruments and singing, holding their own and more in the band, or like Ola Belle, also leading the band, making the rules.

Back around 1980 I was in Nashville and had a long, bizarre conversation with Roni Stoneman (part of which was about my split with Mike) at some function or other. She finished the conversation with "All men are shit asses. I don't play the banjo much any more. I could get more out of picking my nose." Never one to shy away from any topic, there was another statement she made—and this went straight into my 1981 diary writing about that evening: "She had her uterus bronzed and it will be in the Jim Reeves Museum!" Truth is stranger than fiction. Turns out Roni talked about the bronze uterus in the book *Pressing On: The Roni Stoneman Story* (2007). She didn't say anything about the Jim Reeves Museum though, and apparently the museum doesn't exist anymore, although it seems that the artifacts may have been acquired by a collector. Roni continued to play and perform, including with her sister Donna at the 2021 Stoneman Family's induction into the IBMA Hall of Fame. She died in 2024.

Most often the women like Wilma Lee Cooper and Ola Belle Reed, who were strong players and band emcees, played in bands with their husbands or other family members. There weren't many who did it on their own. One who did was Cynthia May Carver (1903–80), known professionally as "Cousin Emmy," a "brassy and outspoken" blonde bombshell from Barren County, Kentucky, who played banjo, fiddle, harmonica, and, famously, a rubber surgeon's glove. She'd inflate it with air and, when it was full, let the air out gradually pulling on the fingers, squeaking out "You Are My Sunshine"—all while dressed in a tight black dress with a long side slit, spike heel shoes, and upswept white-blonde hair. In the 1930s, she toured around on her own, playing radio stations and making personal appearances. Cousin Emmy was a guest on an episode of Pete Seeger's *Rainbow Quest* television show, and there are quite a few recordings by her that survive. Later on, Cousin Emmy moved to L.A. and worked some in the movies, and adopted and raised several children—on her own.

Another was Gloria Flickinger, a young woman whom I remember would often come to Sunset Park with her mother. From Hanover,

Pennsylvania, she was a good musician and singer, playing banjo, guitar, bass, and mandolin quite well. And she wanted to play so badly she could taste it. She would come to the park with her mother and the first thing she'd do would be to go up to whoever was featured that day and ask them if she could get up and play, to make a "guest appearance." I never heard of anyone turning her down. And she worked hard to forge a career in music, entering contests, finding work with various bands, honing her skills, on the way to becoming Gloria Belle, eventually joining Jimmy Martin's band around 1968. She played snare drum, bass, occasionally mandolin as well as singing, working with him off and on for a decade. I was horrified that Jimmy treated her with such disrespect. It was bizarre, and many of us have wondered how she could stand working for him. During a set he was openly mean and sexist toward her, making jokes about her singing, playing, the way she looked—everything was fair game. Maybe she figured it was the price of admission. As Hazel once put it about some of her tough times playing as the "chick singer" in local bluegrass bands during the late 1950s, "I put up with that shit just so I could get to play."

Women musicians in bluegrass were rare in the 1950s, and if they didn't have cover with husbands or family in the band, they were vulnerable. This was the case with Gloria Belle. She mostly ignored Jimmy's antics and put up with a lot of crap because like Hazel, she just wanted to play the music—she was driven to play. And she did. Through the years she played and toured with many bands, including several "all girl" bands that she formed. Murphy Henry's book *Pretty Good for a Girl: Women in Bluegrass* offers some insight from Gloria herself: "[Jimmy] was afraid to praise his band members for fear they would 'let down.' I wouldn't argue with him. The more I could ignore it the better it was."

One very notable family group, Alec Campbell and Ola Belle Campbell Reed, performed regularly at New River Ranch and Sunset Park, where they were the host band for more than twenty-five years. Originally from Ashe County, North Carolina, the two had moved north with their musical family during the Depression and settled near Rising Sun, Maryland. They soon formed the New River Gang, playing local shows as well as starting a weekly live radio show, *Campbell's Corner*, featuring bluegrass and country music.

PARK LIFE, FESTIVALS, AND OTHER GATHERINGS

Bluegrass music is marginal music now, but it was *really* marginal back in 1950s and '60s. Even after *The Beverly Hillbillies* show hit in 1962, bringing media attention to Lester Flatt and Earl Scruggs in particular and bluegrass in general, it was still hard going for most. Musicians traveled constantly, worked hard, and didn't make a lot of money. The fans knew all the songs and tunes, forgave their idols when they weren't at their best, appreciated their best, and thought of them as family and neighbors. There was an informality; there were no snow fences or barriers separating audience from performers, no backstage passes needed, no assigned seating, no separation of haves from have-nots. Once at Sunset Park, Bill Monroe (a big baseball fan) and his band started a game in the field behind the stage during a break.

Gloria Flickinger, who became better known professionally as Gloria Belle, entered the annual banjo contest at New River Ranch near Rising Sun, Maryland, with her mother backing her on guitar, 1956 or '57. A Gibson Mastertone banjo was first prize. Photo by Jeremy Foster; courtesy Alice Gerrard.

Bluegrass festivals have become commonplace these days with hundreds of them in the United States and throughout the United Kingdom and Europe. The very first bluegrass festival in the United States was a one-day event started by guitarist and singer Bill Clifton. Gradually, these one-day events morphed into two-day weekend festivals, which were more extravagant versions of the park shows. Still mainly in large rural areas, people set up campsites or parked campers and trailers and became ensconced for the weekend, immersing themselves in day and night-long jam sessions with occasional breaks to go to the stage to catch performances by their favorite artists. Like the park shows, these early days of bluegrass festivals were informal (almost always white) gatherings filled with jamming, reconnecting with friends, and making new connections, with young enthusiasts often recording the shows, and I often taking photos. But mostly it was all about the music.

Bill Monroe and band onstage at the Indian Springs Bluegrass Festival near Hagerstown, Maryland, ca. 1972.

Typical audience at a bluegrass festival, ca. 1959.
Photo by Jeremy Foster; courtesy Alice Gerrard.

Typically, the music parks were set in clearings in wooded areas, or at the edge of a field, sometimes the stage would be covered, sometimes not. Sometimes there'd be a small backstage area with stairs that led down behind the stage, but just as likely only the rickety stairs. Audiences sat on rough wooden plank benches set among the trees or in the field. New River Ranch was more primitive than Sunset Park, with planks laid across cinder blocks, amid a grove of trees, a makeshift stage against a creek, and a couple of outhouses. Sound systems were basic—those were the days when bands usually gathered around one mic. Sunset Park was a bit different in that the audience members on the plank benches were covered by a kind of open-sided shelter, and the stage was more substantial, with small rooms off to the back.

The parks were set up like a small-town carnival with booths that had games where you might win a stuffed animal; food vendors with pickled eggs, hot dogs and hamburgers, and cotton candy; and there was the rickety Ferris wheel for the brave children to ride. We'd often invite the Stanley Brothers or Bill Monroe or various band members to share in our picnic. Touring musicians got tired of restaurant food and appreciated some good home cooking and a chance to catch up on how the family was, who was sick, who had died, and who was still working the farm or at the factory, mill, grocery store, or garage.

The parks are mostly gone now. Sunset Park, at the intersection of Baltimore Pike and Route 796, closed in 1993. A shopping center covers the field where parking and jamming lived, and a retirement community sits where music was made. Hopefully folks can still hear echoes of Wilma Lee, Ola Belle, Bill Monroe, Stanley Brothers, and dozens of others breaking through cracks in the cement, wafting through the air, making its way to them like in the old days.

New River Ranch banjo contest, 1956 or '57. One of a very few women competing on banjo (or on anything) was Louise Foreacre, who lived near Elkton, Maryland. Originally from North Carolina, she was one of the many transplants who moved to that area of Pennsylvania and Maryland. In 1997 or thereabouts Mike Seeger gathered together a collection of his old field recordings for a Smithsonian Folkways project, *Close to Home*. His recording of Ms. Foreacre playing "Shout Little Lulu" is on this wonderful compilation. Photo by Jeremy Foster; courtesy Alice Gerrard.

Springing up all over the United States in the late 1950s and '60s, folk festivals had an overlap in audience with the bluegrass and old-time music park events, but with a different vibe. In addition to the slew of festivals in the Northeast, the Chicago Folk Festival, started in 1960, is still going strong. From the Berkeley Folk Festival (1958–70) to several Canadian folk festivals—Winnipeg, Mariposa, Toronto—and a myriad of others, festivals popped up across North America. The musicians and craftspeople at the festivals were diverse culturally and racially—from different backgrounds, often from different countries, and they were thrown together for long weekends, sometimes a week or two, housed in college dormitories, in homes, sometimes taking over a whole hotel. The participants got to know one another, or renew friendships, trade stories and experiences, enjoy each other's company, and appreciate their commonalities as well as their differences. In the living room of the house where we were all staying at the 1982 World's Fair in Knoxville, Tennessee, two great fiddlers—New York City Irishman Brendan Mulvahill and North Carolinian Tommy Jarrell, along with bluegrass mandolin player Roland White—shared tunes, stories, and lots of laughs in the evenings after the days' work was done at the fair. Virginia bluegrass musician Smiley Hobbs struck up a friendship with idiosyncratic Bahamian singer and guitar player Joseph Spence at the Newport Folk Festival in 1966, taking huge delight in Spence's music. I'll never forget the sight of seventy-something Nimrod Workman, ex–coal miner and singer from Kentucky and West Virginia, trading moves with the teenage African American downtown DC breakdancers at one of the Smithsonian Folklife Festival after-parties, blowing their minds and winning their approval as he joined them on the dance floor. With a gleam and a twinkle in his deep-set black eyes, "Nim" suddenly dropped to the ground in a squat, threw his skinny arms behind his skinny legs and crab walked across the dance floor to much hooting and hollering and dropped jaws. The kids loved it and so did Nim. There were many such moments to treasure.

Ralph Rinzler and Jim Morris conceived of and developed the Smithsonian Festival of American Folklife, which first took place on DC's National Mall in 1967 over the Fourth of July weekend. It is an amazing event, still going strong and open to the public. It presents music and other folk traditions like basket weaving, spinning yarn, dance, and more. A boat or cabin might be built, fishing nets woven, or dolls made, often with music accompanying the work. The great singer Norman Kennedy, a master weaver originally from Aberdeen, Scotland, sang his wonderful songs and "mouth music" fiddling while he wove. I remember the eerie, beautiful sounds of the fife and drumming of

TOP Newport (Rhode Island) Folk Festival, 1966. The great Bahamian guitarist and singer Joseph Spence (*left*) with Smiley Hobbs from Manassas, Virginia. Smiley was knocked out and intrigued by Spence's music (as many are). Smiley, a wonderful musician, had come up to play banjo with Hazel and me at the festival.

BOTTOM Willard Watson (*left*) and his cousin Doc Watson (*right*). Willard was a wonderful flatfoot dancer, woodcarver, banjo player, and storyteller. He was not as universally known as Doc, but those who got to see and hear Willard in action will never forget him.

Ed and Lonnie and G. D. Young from Mississippi as they snaked along low to the ground, bent and twisting as they made their way along the mall, and the insistent, powerful slide playing and singing of Muddy Waters. And so many others.

At that first Folklife Festival in 1967, we gathered near one of the museums and suddenly the Olympia Brass Band from Louisiana struck up a tune and started marching down the street and on the mall, weaving through the tourists and folks on their way to work or going about their business. Everyone was taken by surprise and thrilled, and followed along behind the band, winding along the grassy mall between the Reflecting Pool and the Washington Monument.

The Newport Folk Festival in Rhode Island was first conceived of by George Wein, who had founded the Newport Jazz Festival. With the help of Pete Seeger and entrepreneur and folk and rock manager Albert Grossman, Wein organized the first two-day Newport Folk Festival in 1959 with a lineup that included Pete Seeger, Sonny Terry and Brownie McGhee, the Kingston Trio, Earl Scruggs, Joan Baez, and the New Lost City Ramblers, among others. According to writer Rick Massimo, in

Smithsonian Folklife Festival, 1968. Bessie Jones (*left*) talking with Elizabeth Cotten (*right*) in the backstage area.

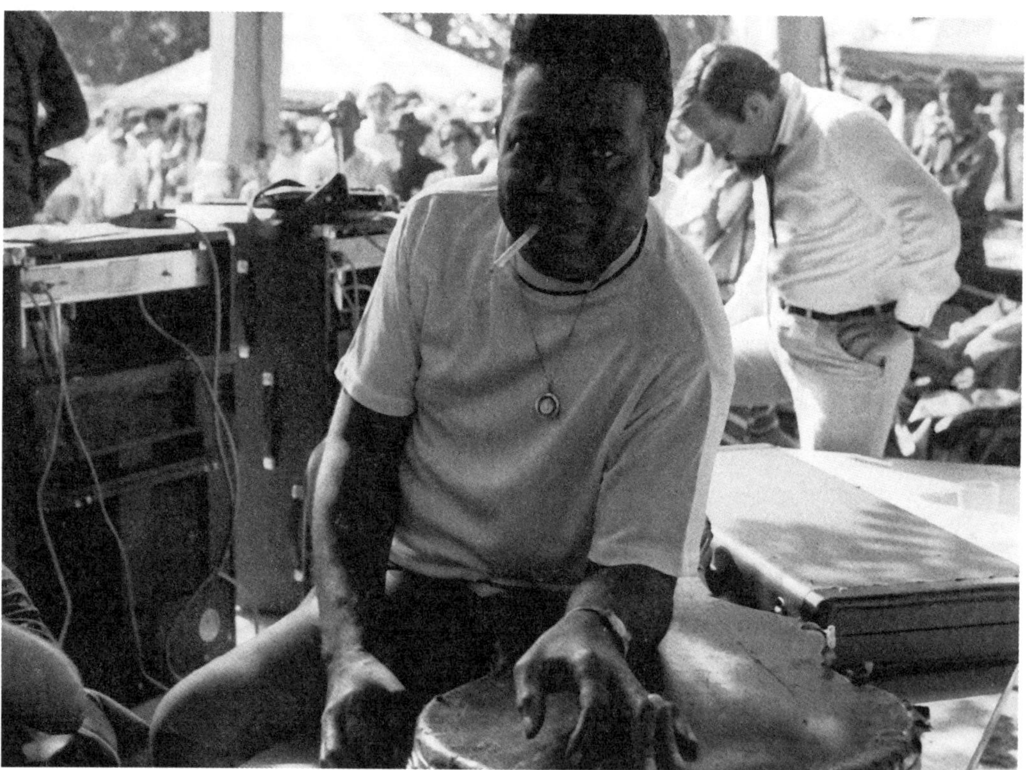

TOP Smithsonian Folklife Festival, 1968. The Georgia Sea Island Singers mixing it up with Ed and Lonnie Young of the Mississippi Fife and Drum band.

BOTTOM McKinley Morganfield (Muddy Waters) at the Smithsonian Folklife Festival, 1968 or '69.

1962 a board of directors, "representative of every branch of the folk world," and the nonprofit Newport Folk Foundation were formed with a mission to showcase the diversity of American folk music. Performers were paid fifty dollars per day—union scale at that time—regardless of their commercial stature. Often bigger-name performers would refuse the pay and cover their own expenses.

In 1966, Hazel and I got invited to perform at Newport as part of the afternoon "new faces" concert on the main stage. We asked Smiley Hobbs to come with us to play banjo and Tex Logan to play fiddle. (I don't remember why Lamar Grier didn't play with us, as he was our usual banjo player—probably he had to work.) I played guitar and Hazel played bass. Smiley was a sheriff in Manassas County, Virginia, and played around the DC area a lot with various bluegrass bands. Mike Seeger recorded him in 1957 for the seminal Folkways vinyl *American Banjo Tunes & Songs in Scruggs Style.* We drove up with Smiley and were naively shocked when we discovered he was carrying a gun in the glove compartment. Musician Jody Stecher remembered that "decades later, Hazel Dickens told me about the trip up to Newport from DC with Smiley Hobbs . . . and Smiley getting angry with someone, maybe a security guard at Newport," and Hazel worrying that there might be a set-to.

Hazel and I got through our performance with no major fuckups, although I don't remember much except that we were nervous as cats. The performance was recorded and appears on several anthology recordings. At Newport, there were many opportunities for socializing and sharing music among the musicians who were often housed together in big old Newport homes. These encounters often led to sweet friendships, like with Smiley Hobbs and Joseph Spence, and occasional flare ups mostly due to too much liquor.

On the opposite end of the festival spectrum was the Pipestem Festival. Set in the mountains of Southern West Virginia, it was a small, rural folklife festival organized in 1968 by Don West (1906–92) with the help of his daughter, banjoist and folksinger Hedy West (1938–2005). Don was a poet and the son of Georgia sharecroppers. He was a trade union organizer, civil rights activist, and cofounder of Tennessee's Highlander Folk School with Myles Horton. In 1964, Don and his wife Connie established the Appalachian South Folklife Center in the mountains near the Pipestem community in Summers County, West Virginia. According to Mary Ellen Griffith, chair emerita of the board of directors for the Folklife Center after thirty years of service, "When Don arrived in West Virginia he went about meeting local musicians and craftspeople to teach at the [center]. With [Hedy's] help he produced the first festival with musicians from around West Virginia and

Appalachia. He was adamant that the performers stick to 'old time' or folk music. [Two young musicians from Ivydale, West Virginia,] John and Dave Morris, were at that festival and subsequent ones for many years after that. Dave often credited Don for encouraging him to produce the very popular festival they held at Ivydale, West Virginia, for several years."

The Pipestem Festival brought together local musicians both Black and white, was strictly homemade, put together with love, hard work, and an idealism for representing local culture, transcending barriers through music. At the 1969 Pipestem Festival that Mike Seeger and I went to, there was some great music performed on a small, rickety stage by local musicians mostly gone now. I loved the fact that it was so regional, a cooperative effort by young people and old people, people who cared about their community and knew that all politics is local. I took lots of photos.

Organized by the Brandywine Friends of Old-Time Music in 1974, the Brandywine Mountain Music Convention was somewhere in between Pipestem and a larger folk festival. Held outdoors near Brandywine, Delaware, for twenty years, the weekend festival presented traditional musicians and dancers from around the country; people camped and jammed and listened to music all weekend. Since it was more or less in her backyard, Ola Belle Reed and her family were there very often in some capacity or other. She became the grande dame of the Brandywine Festival and its spiritual matriarch in a sense. My friend and fellow musician Beverly Smith gave a nice description of the festival to the Field Recorders Collective in 2015:

> There used to be this great festival where we would all meet, which we just called Brandywine. And it was a wonderful, wonderful festival . . . [and] they used to bring out really great old players . . . they would feature different areas of the US every year. There was West Virginia one year, and they'd bring up all these old fiddlers from West Virginia. They did Virginia, Texas. . . . It was not only a great place to get to play with everybody but also to hear these old guys play. . . . Brandywine was one of those places where you'd get to play for people who actually understood the music, listened to the music, loved the music. Most places that a band like ours would play, it's sort of like introducing people to old-time music. It's really great to play for people that know it and love it.

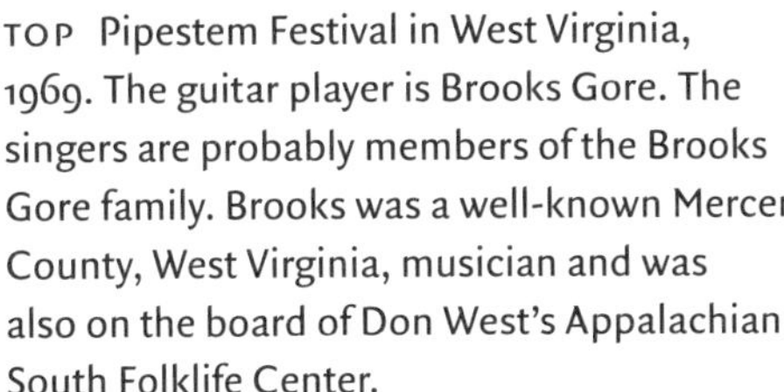

TOP Pipestem Festival in West Virginia, 1969. The guitar player is Brooks Gore. The singers are probably members of the Brooks Gore family. Brooks was a well-known Mercer County, West Virginia, musician and was also on the board of Don West's Appalachian South Folklife Center.

BOTTOM LEFT Pipestem Festival, 1969. Local singer and piano and guitar player Earl Gilmore from the Black coal camp at Clinchco, Virginia, with photographer Rick Diehl.

BOTTOM RIGHT Pipestem Festival, 1969. Banjo player Jenes Cottrell from Clay County, West Virginia.

The National Council for the Traditional Arts sponsored Liberty Weekend, a festival in Manhattan, held adjacent to the harbor as part of the Centennial weekend celebration. Earnest East and the Pine Ridge Boys & Patsy from Surry County, North Carolina, were invited to play. The National Folk Festival, founded in 1934 by Sarah Gertrude Knott, and held at different locations throughout the years, was held in Vienna, Virginia, at Wolf Trap Farm from 1971 to 1982.

Festivals like Newport, Smithsonian, and Pipestem always tried to bring the whole picture of American traditional music to people, including diverse music from different parts of the country. Showing the influences of Black music on white music in the South was of huge importance.

The South was slow to acknowledge the Black influence on the music that existed everywhere in the South—that the music was a combination of primarily African American—brought here by enslaved Africans—and

Earl Gilmore at the Pipestem Festival, 1969. I can still hear his powerful, keening voice, feeling every note and turn.

Anglo-American traditions, as well as the many influences of migrants: German, French, and others, and of course the first people who lived here, the Native Americans. But the Black-white mix is what gives Southern music, in my opinion, its uniqueness—those musical moments with their slurs, syncopation, improvisation, and more are at its essence. A few important white musicians like Bill Monroe would talk about Arnold Schulz, a Black guitar player who was a big influence on him, or Maybelle Carter, who acknowledged Lesley Riddle, a Black guitar player, as an influence on her playing. But talking about race didn't get into the conversation a lot. And the banjo, always held up as the quintessential American instrument invented by white people, had, in fact, been introduced to the South by enslaved Africans.

THE IMPORTANCE OF THE BLACK BANJO

Lately there has been important growth among young African American musicians in uncovering, understanding, and reclaiming their history of the banjo. In 2004, Tony Thomas, an African American scholar with a particular interest in the real history of the banjo, started a listserv, "Black Banjo Then and Now." He, along with several other banjo history enthusiasts, were driven to explore the banjo's African roots and its transition to the American South via enslaved Africans. It is a complicated history marked by racism, minstrelsy, Jim Crow, Uncle Tom-ism, and a host of other negative stereotypes, culminating in its ultimate rejection by most younger African Americans.

On the listserv, people suggested that there should be an informal conference focusing on the Black banjo. Mark Freed, a member of the listserv, and soon to be head of student programming at Appalachian State University, agreed. So did Cecelia "Cece" Conway, professor of English and Folklore at ASU and author of *African Banjo Echoes in Appalachia* from University of Tennessee Press. With Tony Thomas, musician and banjo historian, they started the wheels rolling and the Black Banjo Gathering was born. Help came from others—Sule Greg Wilson, an African American historian, banjoist, percussionist, and dancer; Rhiannon Giddens, singer, fiddler, and banjoist; and many others. It was open to the public, and the people came. I was at the first one in 2005 where many young (and older) Black musicians got to meet one another for the first time. Joe Thompson (1918–2012) from Mebane, North Carolina, one of the last Black traditional fiddlers still playing, was there; three young African American musicians (strangers to one another at the time), Giddens, Justin Robinson, and Dom Flemons, met Joe for the first time at the Gathering and later visited him often at his home in Mebane to learn as much as they could about his life and music.

Ultimately, Giddens, Robinson, and Flemons formed the Carolina Chocolate Drops, a string band recognized through their recordings, concerts, and workshops as one of the very first groups to empower and bring more light onto the African history of the banjo and the mighty influence of enslaved African musicians on early traditional music in the South, a history mostly forgotten or unrecognized (deliberately or not).

Cheick Hamala Diabate, a ngoni player from West Africa who lived in Maryland, was at the Gathering, and so were Bela Fleck and Abigail Washburn, white American banjo players with a keen interest in banjo history; the Ebony Hillbillies string band from New York City, headed up by Henrique Prince and Norris Washington; Don Vappie, jazz banjoist from New Orleans; Daniel Jatta, a Jola scholar and akonting player from the Gambia, along with his friend Ulf Jagfors, Swedish banjo historian and collector. Algia Mae Hinton from the Piedmont area of North Carolina—banjo and guitar player and buck dancer—was there with her son Willette, also an extraordinary dancer, as were a host of youngish white banjo enthusiasts and players like Mike Seeger, John Cohen, Jim Bollman, Pete Ross, and Greg Adams.

In 2010, when the Black Banjo Gathering reunion was held—again, at Appalachian State—many of the same people were there, in addition to new young Black players like Hubby Jenkins and Jerron Paxton. It is my contention that the 2005 Black Banjo Gathering was the start of the renaissance of young Black players taking back their history and connection to traditional music as well as their ability to make it their own and perhaps take it in different directions. And ultimately it has encouraged organizations like the IBMA to become more inclusive and diverse. I trust this influence will continue, grow, and will make us all better musicians and carriers of tradition. More and more African Americans are involving themselves in spreading the word: people like Dena Jennings and the Affrilachian On-Time Music Gathering in Orange, Virginia; musicians like Giddens; DaShawn Hickman, a pedal steel player from Mount Airy, North Carolina, who learned to play from his mother; and Jake Blount, from Alexandria, Virginia, a multi-instrumentalist and singer; to name just a few. And it might surprise many country music fans to know there was always a Black presence in Nashville country music, from Grand Ole Opry star DeFord

Fiddlers Grove, in Union Grove, North Carolina, 1987 (run by Harper Van Hoy—not the Union Grove Fiddlers Convention, which was run by his brother Pierce Van Hoy). A young and eager Tim Donnelly is playing with one of his music heroes, Enoch Rutherford.

Bailey in the 1920s to Charley Pride in the 1970s. After a regrettable lull, the current scene is diversifying: Queen Esther, Allison Russell, Kane Brown, Brittney Spencer, Mickey Guyton, Darius Rucker, and other African Americans are putting their stamp on the music.

Fiddlers conventions are essentially weekend or one-day music (occasionally week-long) competitions. They exist throughout the country—many of them for years. The National Oldtime Fiddlers Contest in Weiser, Idaho, has been running since 1953. The Galax Fiddlers Convention, one of the oldest and largest in the Southeast, is still held every August, as it has been since 1935. Rules and competition categories vary from convention to convention but essentially include fiddle, banjo, guitar, mandolin, band, autoharp, sometimes dulcimer, and sometimes singing. Money, ribbons, and (sometimes extravagant) designations such as "world champion" are usually awarded. Fiddlers conventions are usually held outdoors in a park, on farmland, or sometimes indoors at a schoolhouse or community center, and again folks generally like to set up camp, forming enclaves of long-running jam sessions, breaking only to eat, perhaps sleep a little, or compete. One of my proudest moments was taking home the "Henry Whitter Memorial Award, Best All-Around Performer, Fries Vol. Fire Dept. Fiddlers Convention, 1983." The plaque sits on my office wall today.

There are fiddlers picnics, much like fiddlers conventions—basically gatherings of musicians but without the competition. People get together in outdoor spaces, play music, have jam sessions, eat, and sometimes perform but in general don't compete.

One of these was the Eighth Annual Alamance County (North Carolina) Fiddlers Picnic held in May 1983 on the grounds of the Alamance County Historical Museum. According to the *Burlington Daily Times-News*, "the picnic will feature old-time string music, traditional arts and crafts, food and drinks, antique photography, horse and buggy rides, cider making and an antique hat and bonnet exhibit."

Tommy Jarrell (*right*) with Andy Cahan at the Alamance County Fiddlers Picnic, 1983. The picnic, a free event near Burlington, North Carolina, took place annually from 1976 to 1987. Situated around the old Holt House, which also served as a museum, the picnic was a fun, welcoming gathering place for musicians and friends.

Another sort of gathering, a combination of camp-out, informal teaching and sharing sessions, all-day and all-night jam sessions, usually over a weekend, was exemplified by Sweets Mill, a bucolic former logging camp set in the Sierra Nevada foothills near Fresno, California, on on 240-plus acres owned by Edith and Virgil Byxbe. Sweets Mill had established itself since the early 1960s as a refuge and gathering place for old-time musicians and dancers, friends, family, and partners mainly from the West Coast—a "hippie haven," loose, cooperative, communal, lots of pot, kind of free-form and friendly.

Mike Seeger and I and three of my children were living in Fresno during the spring of 1974 when Mike undertook a residency teaching a class on American old-time music at Cal State University, Fresno, and we all went to Sweets Mill. I remember that we pitched a tent, maybe did a workshop or two, and generally joined in the fun. There was a lodge where people gathered to eat and jam, and a beautiful pond where there was lots of naked swimming, lots of woods and nooks and crannies where small groups leaned in to share a tune or song. Music and dance were everywhere. I remember waking up early one morning to the hauntingly beautiful sound of Suzy (Rothfield) Thompson sitting by the water singing. No instrument—her powerful voice sailing out through the trees, up the hill, echoing it seemed, throughout the universe. Many memories are hazy, but that one remains strong and clear. (A couple of good books on Sweet's Mill are *The Road to Sweet's Mill: The West Coast Folk Revival in the 1960s and '70s*, by Evo Bluestein [2017], and *At the Mill: The Story of Sweet Mill, California, by, for and about the Folks of Sweets Mill*, compiled and edited by Patty Hall [1975]).

Informal music gatherings can happen at the drop of a hat just about any place—a bar, a room, out in a field, on a porch, a stage. . . . Our music lives anywhere that you have at least one musician with a song or tune to play, or two or more musicians with the desire to make music with one another.

Rev. Frederick Douglass Kirkpatrick at the Poor People's Campaign, Washington, DC, 1968.

Chapter 4

SEARCHING FOR A BETTER WORLD

During the late 1950s and '60s in Washington, DC, there was a lot of civil rights activity, including the 1963 March on Washington, where thousands gathered to hear Dr. Martin Luther King Jr.'s "I Have a Dream" speech. I remember the feeling of community and love for Dr. King and the Poor People's March and Campaign in 1968, held for several weeks on the National Mall, where a tent city—Resurrection City—sprang up to highlight the need for economic justice for poor people. Rev. Frederick Douglass Kirkpatrick, a minister and political activist from Louisiana, also a powerful singer and guitar player involved with the campaign, was visiting my house in DC. I don't remember exactly when this was, but it could have been during the Poor People's Campaign or possibly on his way to perform at the Newport Folk Festival. He was a big man, a former football player, and a powerful presence. I remember that during his visit he sat down at the upright piano in the living room and casually delivered the most sarcastic version of "Old Black Joe" you'd ever want to hear, mocking the nostalgic version of Southern life, the racist longing for the "good old days of good masters and good darkies" so common in many of Stephen Foster's popular songs.

I was living in DC when Dr. King was assassinated and thousands of furious and frustrated people took to the streets, expressing grief and anger with pent-up rage at decades of injustice and systemic racism. Four days of chaos ensued; buildings were burned, stores were looted, and mostly Black people suffered. My record collector friend Dick Spottswood filled my van with supplies and groceries, and we joined others who were delivering to people in the areas most affected.

I hadn't grown up in the South with awareness of the Jim Crow injustice that existed there, but my parents were liberals who brought me up to believe in equality and human rights for all people. As I was becoming interested in folk and traditional music, folk festivals like Newport, Philadelphia, and others were presenting Black as well as white musicians; efforts were made by some to point out the deep connections between Black and white Southern music; to show how the slides and slurs and syncopations of singing and instrumental styles were influenced by African music; how the banjo did not, in fact, originate as a white instrument but was created by enslaved Africans in this country using gourds, skins, gut strings, and the memory of instruments from their homelands—including the akonting and other spiked gourd-lute instruments.

But the truth was that, in the 1960s folk revival, relatively few young Black people were interested in the traditional music of their forebears in the same way that young white people were becoming interested in traditional music. Maybe there were too many associations with slavery, lynching, and Jim Crow? Plus, along with many of their white counterparts, there was often the desire to find new music that more accurately reflected their present experience. This has been changing gradually, and today more and more young African Americans are thinking in terms of reclaiming (and advancing) their places in Southern musical traditions.

THE BEGINNINGS OF THE SFCRP

The civil rights movement was gaining strength in the South at the same time that young middle class, mostly Northern whites were discovering and embracing Southern traditional music. Sometime between 1965 and 1966, an amazing encounter took place in Atlanta between Anne Romaine and Bernice Reagon. Anne was the petite, blond-haired, blue-eyed daughter of a state senator who had come out of poverty to become a lawyer and state legislator. A granddaughter of Gastonia, North Carolina, millworkers, she was now a political activist living in Atlanta. Bernice Johnson Reagon was a soft-featured, African American woman from Albany, Georgia, the daughter of a preacher. Bernice was one of the original Freedom Singers, a political activist, later to become a renowned scholar, and founder of the singing group, Sweet Honey in the Rock, among many accomplishments. Both women had in common great courage, strong determination and will, and a passion for social justice.

As Bernice remembered during a National Public Radio interview in 1994, "I was in my house in Atlanta, Georgia, and somebody knocked on my door. I opened the door and there was this short white woman about my height. She told me she wanted to start a tour, and she wanted the tour to be Black and white singers from the South and did I know how to do it. I said 'Yes.' ' . . . would I help her?' I said 'Okay,' so Anne Romaine and I organized the first tour. She called white institutions she knew and I called black institutions I knew, and it was the first interracial tour of musicians in the South."

The idea for such a tour emerged during a conference Anne attended at the Highlander Folk School in the fall of 1965. Highlander, located near Knoxville, Tennessee, was noted for its leadership training of civil rights activists. Bob Moses (1935–2021), civil rights giant, Student Nonviolent Coordinating Committee (SNCC) leader, and cofounder of the Mississippi Freedom Democratic Party, was at this meeting at Highlander along with leaders and staffers representing many facets of the civil rights organizations operating in the South. Bob suggested that the impecunious young Southern Student Organizing Committee might try to raise money by using sympathetic folk singers like Bob Dylan and Joan Baez, just as SNCC had done, and it caught Anne's attention.

After her discussions with Bernice Johnson Reagon, however, the concept was modified. In his book *Just My Soul Responding: Rhythm and Blues, Black Consciousness, and Race Relations*, Brian Ward tells us that instead of bringing in Northern-based folk celebrities, "[they]

Newport Folk Festival, 1968. Bernice Reagon with Norman Kennedy and Merle Watson (*right*) and Fred McDowell (?) (*left*).

—Moran Lee "Dock" Boggs—

Moran Lee "Dock" Boggs (1898–1971) was a banjo player and singer from Norton, Virginia, a former coal miner who had recorded commercially during the 1920s and was "rediscovered" by Mike Seeger in the 1960s, who recorded him for Folkways Records. He was a mainstay of the SFCRP tours. Influenced by African American musicians he heard in the mines and on the railroads around where he lived, Dock was known for his masterful bluesy renditions of such songs as "Down South Blues," "Sugar Baby," "Country Blues," "Pretty Polly," "Hard Luck Blues," and many more.

Dock had a special relationship with Anne. Letters between the two reflected their mutual respect and admiration. Arrangements for bus travel, fees agreed upon, monies owed, etc. were all dealt with in formal fashion via letters back and forth in the late 1960s. From Anne:

> *I don't believe that I ever wrote to tell you how much I enjoyed my overnight visit with you all last month. It was a real pleasure for me. My mouth still waters when I think about that good breakfast we had. Also I was so glad to meet you, Mrs. Boggs. Dock has said*

Blackey, Kentucky, fall 1968. Dock Boggs in the community center playing for a group of intent teenagers. Accompanying him on guitar is John Kaparakis (d. 2020), a Washington, DC, friend.

so many nice things about you and always speaks of you in such a loving way.

Dock, the tour begins on Saturday October 26 in Asheville, N.C. at Montreat-Anderson College. Could you stay with the tour for at least a week? We may need you for a few days more. . . . Could you ride the bus to Asheville? If you could ride the bus to Asheville or the train, I could have someone meet you there and we would of course pay the bus fare. . . . Again, the salary will be $150 for each week plus all of your room and board and transportation.

Your friend,
Anne Romaine.

Dock replied:

I'll leave Norton to make it in over at Asheville NC 26 Oct. Please have some one to meet me if Mike can't pick me up. I wish to know the schedule and know what is expected of me. If serious sickness doesn't prevail you can count on me.

I hope you and Howard [Anne's husband] are in good health and prosper, may God's richest blessings rest upon you. Please take all misspellt words and mistakes for my friendship and love. God Bless you both. Poor Dock and Wife.

Norton, Virginia, 1968. During one of the SFCRP tours we stopped at Dock's home and I took a photo of him getting coal from his coal shed.

would use local southern musicians [both Black and white] to dramatize and celebrate a common, essentially working-class heritage of struggle against poverty and injustice through the various indigenous musics of the region" and that they "held that the traditional blues, folk and country musics of the southern states, with their wonderfully chaotic maelstrom of cross-racial influence and counter-influence, could be used to highlight the deep interpenetration and manifold similarities of black and white experiences in the region while still preserving respect for the distinctiveness of each."

During this time traditional music was enjoying a sort of renaissance in the North among young college students through the Newport Folk Festival, Israel Young's Folklore Center in Manhattan, Harry Smith's Anthology of American Folk Music recordings, Club 47 (now Club Passim) in Cambridge, Massachusetts, the 2nd Fret in Philadelphia, through Pete Seeger, the New Lost City Ramblers, and others. But in the South, its home, it was losing ground to rock 'n' roll and pop music. Taken for granted and unappreciated at best, and denigrated as "too hillbilly" at worst, its practitioners mostly played for themselves, if they played at all. When Northern enthusiasts began to search for and find the legendary musicians they had heard on 78 recordings and Harry Smith's *Anthology of American Folk Music*—Dock Boggs, Maybelle Carter, and Mississippi John Hurt, and others—they were spirited away up north to perform. Thus began, for many of them, a career rebirth and a growing appreciation by young audiences. They were sought after, young people wanted to learn their music and would "sit at the feet of the masters." But this career rebirth, for the most part, took place away from their home communities, and the plan that Anne and Bernice had, to present traditional music in the South, to Southerners, was a unique one in the mid-1960s. Ward calls this "a truly unprecedented event. It had political and cultural, as well as artistic motives—to help create an appreciation among southerners for their own music, and to reflect back, through music and the people who sang and played the music, southern culture and the struggles of the working-class South."

Anne dove in. Bernice knew musicians and Anne was a go-getter in terms of organizing and carrying through on a plan, and both were committed. "I just wrote hundreds and hundreds of letters," said Anne, "and set up this tour and Bernice got Reverend Pearly Brown [a blind African American street singer from Americus, Georgia] . . . and Mabel Hillary [an African American singer, also from Georgia] . . . Hedy West [a white singer, born in north Georgia, the daughter of labor activist Don West] . . . and we traveled around the South in this Volkswagen bus."

The Southern Festival of Song, as it was known in April 1966, was the first of many tours to travel throughout the South, performing on college campuses, in community centers, and at rallies or political events. As the first brochure from the Southern Festival of Song read, "The answer to existence in today's world lies in the ability of man to accentuate his common bonds, setting them up as lines of communication with others. . . . Tonight, we would like to show that in America, one of these common bonds lies in our grassroots music. In spite of the fact that many of us have existed for years at opposite poles on many issues, when it comes to music, we draw freely from each other."

The first Southern Festival of Song roster included luminaries like Deford Bailey, Rev. Pearly Brown, Johnny Cash, Mable Hillery, and more, and was held in Neely Auditorium at Vanderbilt University on April 22, 1966, sponsored by the Vanderbilt Student Christian Association. Eventually, the Southern Festival of Song became the nonprofit Southern Folk Cultural Revival Project (SFCRP), and while Bernice went on to pursue other musical and academic avenues, the SFCRP was a major part of Anne Romaine's life and continued under her leadership until her untimely death due to a ruptured appendix in 1995.

Hazel and I joined the tour in 1967. By this time, there were usually two tours each year, one in the Mountain South and one in the Deep South. We would drive to Nashville or Atlanta where Anne was living and join up with the others who would arrive, usually by bus if we didn't pick them up en route. We'd head off in Anne's or my van—ready for anything—taking turns driving, crisscrossing the South and landing in places like Charlotte College; Brevard College; Somerset Community College; Blackey, Kentucky; the University of Virginia; Memphis State; Big Stone Gap; Auburn University; and Guilford College, just to name a few. There would usually be five or six of us, with occasional others meeting us along the way for a concert or two. We all sat onstage together, taking turns playing and singing, supporting one another. The times on the road were fun, exciting, often arduous, sometimes tense when tempers would flare or we'd grow tired of always being together in such close quarters—but always inspiring and wonderful. We bounced around the Mountain South (usually in the fall) and the Deep South (usually in the spring), always on a financial shoestring.

We slept in motels or in college dormitories if we were lucky but were often jammed onto a couch in someone's living room. I remember sharing a bed with Elizabeth Cotten one night. Just as I'd drift off to sleep, she'd start to snore; I'd nudge her, she'd quit, I'd drift off again, and she'd start up again. A night to remember. But it *was* Elizabeth Cotten.

TOP On tour, probably in Pike County, Kentucky, 1971. (*Left to right*) Hazel Dickens, Jack Wright, Kilby Snow, Rich Kirby, and unknown man with child.

BOTTOM Getting ready to load up the van, ca. 1968. (*Left to right*) Babe Stovall, Red Parham, Bill McElreath, Hazel Dickens, and Elizabeth Cotten behind Rev. Pearly Brown.

Elizabeth Cotten

Elizabeth Cotten was an African American guitarist, singer, and composer ("Freight Train," "Shake Sugaree," and others). Left-handed, she played a right-handed guitar in a fingerpicked style and was considered one of its premiere exponents. Originally from Carrboro, North Carolina, she learned to play guitar and banjo as a child. When she moved to Washington, DC, she got work as a domestic in the Charles and Ruth Seeger household, where, inevitably, the Seeger children, Mike and Peggy, discovered her talent, and over time through touring and recording she became known to the rest of the world.

Elizabeth often toured with the SFCRP, and she and Dock Boggs struck up a great friendship. They would sit together in the van and talk about life (which they had both lived mightily), religion (wherein they brooked no hypocrites), morality (nonjudgmental), and much more. I wish I'd had a tape recorder. Elizabeth ("Libba") would stash Dock's whiskey flask in her purse for him, and he always helped her in and out of the van and called her "Miss Elizabeth." Elizabeth had an impish sense of humor, and would often get the giggles when we were all onstage, as she remembered something that struck her funny bone—like the time

during a concert she left for a bathroom break, and when she came back, sat down, but then kept kind of giggling to herself trying not to be obvious, and when I got a chance to ask she told me she'd pulled down her brown stockings or leggings and forgot to include the underpants when she hoisted the stockings up. The underpants were down around her legs inside the pulled-up stockings, and there was nothing to do until the concert was over, which it soon was. She was so tickled at what she'd done. I'll bet there are plenty out there who've done the same thing.

FACING Blackey, Kentucky, 1968. The SFCRP stopped to do a workshop in the community center where Elizabeth Cotten played for some young folks. Better known for her guitar playing, Elizabeth also played the banjo.

ABOVE Davidson, North Carolina, 1968. Libba and Hazel checking out a cornhusk doll that one of them bought.

Although we seldom encountered overt hostility as a mixed racial group (nobody chased us with guns or tried to force us off the road) we were very aware of the possibilities of violence or intimidation. We always made sure that when we stopped to eat, we mixed it up in our seating, we were vigilant in supporting one another, in paying attention to our surroundings and listening especially to what the Black members of the tour smelled, saw, heard, and felt. If Bessie Jones or Johnny Shines didn't want to stop at a particular place, we didn't. If Larry Johnson was freaked out about being back in the South after growing up in New York City, we cut him slack. If Elizabeth Cotten muttered, "Those people are watching us," we took her seriously.

There was one incident that will forever be with me, a story that I tell often; the images are so clear in my memory. The van had broken down in some city—Charleston, South Carolina, I believe. We stopped in the mid-afternoon to get the van fixed and checked into a motel. Anne and I went walking around looking for a place to get something to eat and came across a small, empty restaurant and bar. Walking in, we asked the man behind the counter—the owner, I suspect, a big, beefy, ruddy-faced man sporting an apron—if we could get something to eat.

He said "Sure" and left for the kitchen. We sat down in a booth to wait and soon saw our tour-mate Johnny Shines—a blues player and singer from Tennessee and Alabama—also looking for something to eat. We waved him in and asked him to sit with us as the owner came from the kitchen. We told him that our friend had just joined us and could he get a sandwich as well. The owner paused and then said, "I can make him a sandwich, but he'll have to take it out to eat. Y'all can eat yours in here."

In an instant, Anne was on her feet, long blonde hair flying, blue eyes blazing. She marched her five-foot-one self up to the six-foot-plus beefy owner, who was momentarily taken aback by the sight of this "flower" of Southern womanhood suddenly become a pissed-off Southern wild woman, shaking her finger in his face and in a voice that every child remembers as mama's "gonna whip you" voice shouted out at him: "You son of a bitch, that's against the law and I'll have the FBI on your ass so fast you won't know what hit you!"

Rev. Pearly Brown & Babe Stovall

Rev. Pearly Brown (1915–86) from Abbeville, Georgia, was blind from birth. His father had run off and his mother died when he was young. Reverend Brown referred to himself as a "stray child." Raised by "white folks" and by his grandparents, he learned many of the gospel and slave songs he sang from his grandmother, who was a major influence on him. He got interested in playing guitar as a student in the Georgia Academy for the Blind in Macon, which he attended for four years. He made a living with his music, playing and singing on the streets of Macon for most of his life, and performing at folk festivals and other venues. He had weekly radio shows on WDEC in Americus and WIBB in Macon for many years. Reverend Brown almost always came with us on Anne's tours. With his powerful singing and strong personality, he had a gift for

Union Grove, North Carolina, 1967. On the SFCRP tour we stopped at the Union Grove Fiddlers Convention. We were an integrated group, and there were several unsavory characters possibly going to start some trouble. Jewell "Babe" Stovall jumped out of the car and totally defused any tension by performing some of his trick guitar playing behind his head. Me? Mike Seeger?

Babe Stovall (*left*) and Reverend Brown having one of their friendly arguments, Davidson, North Carolina, 1968. They would often argue about the nature of the soul, but also they just loved to "devil" each other, as some called it. And I think it helped pass the time on the road as well.

drawing audiences in and engaging them. Frederick Burger quoted Reverend Brown in an article in the April 1973 issue of *Georgia Magazine*: "I've come to love the street. . . . One of the main things I've learned on the street is to love everybody. You got to overlook how people can be mean to you sometimes. . . . The [Georgia Academy for the Blind] learned me the letter, but I learned the common sense when I got on the street. That's the best of all, common sense and judgement."

As with Dock, Anne had a particularly close relationship to Reverend Brown and always included him on the tours if he could go. After his first time with the tour in 1966, Anne wrote a letter home to Reverend Brown and his wife Christine:

> *I want to tell you how much we enjoyed Rev. Brown on the trip around the South. He really seemed to make a hit almost everywhere we went. He stole the show in North Carolina. In Virginia they are trying to get him back in June. Mrs. Brown, I wish you could have been with us. I think what we were trying to do through music is very important to helping people in the South to understand each other. . . .*
>
> *I hope your trip to Americus on the bus wasn't too bad. I really felt bad about that. It probably would have been better if we had driven in the car the next morning. Thank you for going with us [on] the tour. I'm so glad I got to know you and I learned so much from you. I'm afraid that I gave you some difficult times because of my own lack of confidence as we were driving around the South. This was unnecessary and I am very much ashamed of my own frailties. I don't think it will happen again, as I've learned a great deal from you as well as Bernice and Mable. I hope you will go with us again next year.*

Reverend Brown wrote back letting Anne know that his wife would be coming with him: "She is looking forward to seeing you all. And I really want to see Pete Seeger. . . . And we will leave Thursday the 30th morning at 7 o'clock and will arrive in Atlanta at 11 o'clock. On the Trailways Bus."

Jewell "Babe" Stovall (1907–74) was a blues singer and guitarist from Mississippi who was often on the tour. Used to entertaining crowds as a street musician, he would often play his National steel guitar up behind his neck.

Babe and Reverend Brown had a close relationship. Babe "saw to" Reverend Brown, helping him in and out of the van, walking with him. . . . They often got into heated arguments around the subject of religion, especially as regarded the nature of the soul. Reverend Brown would get very agitated trying to get his point across. I actually taped one of their discussions—very badly recorded and hard to understand but nevertheless it rests in the Southern Folklife Collection somewhere.

Startled, he reached behind the kitchen door, grabbed a broom, raised it over his head and came at her (definitely overkill). Anne was prepared to go full frontal when Johnny stepped in and said, "C'mon, let's get out of here," realizing of course, that he'd be the one to bear the brunt if the confrontation continued and the law came. So we left. Anne called the SBI when we got back to the motel, adding, "I'll bet they won't do anything." We had to leave early the next morning, and I don't remember hearing whether they did or didn't pursue the establishment.

Many of the road warriors who endured the highs and lows of the tours were older musicians; it wasn't easy for them, but I believe that they came along so often because they enjoyed being together, being treated fairly, playing in the South, and also believed we were all working toward something good, something better.

Often Hazel's and my drive to join the tour started along Route 11 (what is now I-81). This very poignant sign (ca. 1971) was on a wall of the Elliston Truck Stop in Elliston, Virginia, south of Roanoke.

A break from the road tour, ca. 1974–75. (*Left to right*) Johnny Shines, Dewey Balfa, Anne Romaine, Rodney Balfa, Mable Hillery, Hazel Dickens, and me. Photo by Cory Foster.

A partial list of other musicians who participated in the tours over the years includes Bessie Jones, Roscoe Holcomb, Red Parham & Bill McElreath, Mable Hillery, Rodney & Dewey Balfa, Ora & Arley Watson, Babe Stovall, Ola Belle and Bud Reed, Sparky Rucker, Drink Small, Lily May Ledford, Mike Seeger, Hedy West, Ralph Stanley, Nimrod Workman, John D. Loudermilk, the Blue Ridge Mountain Dancers, Hazel Dickens, Jane Sapp, Larry Johnson, and many more. Year after year, we would crowd into the van and chase after a better world. It's amazing to think, now, about who took part in these tours and what a powerful experience it was. I can't tell you how much I wish I'd taken more photographs, and how thankful I am that I took as many as I did.

My daughter Cory got permission from her high school to come along on the tour for a week, turning it into a photo project. She took lots of photos during her time with us.

BLACKEY, KENTUCKY

The "War on Poverty" was the backdrop to much of what the SFCRP was doing. Introduced in the early 1960s by President Lyndon Johnson as part of his Great Society initiative, many of the connections Anne made were those of volunteers active in the programs like VISTA, Job Corps, and others "attempting to eliminate poverty by improving living conditions for residents of low-income neighborhoods and by helping the poor access economic opportunities long denied them." The volunteers and other activists lived in the communities in which they were working and had a pretty good handle on what was needed to help fulfill the mission.

One of the communities the tour visited often in the mid to late 1960s and '70s was a small mountain community named Blackey nestled in the mountains of Eastern Kentucky in Letcher County, an area rich in coal, on the north fork of the Kentucky River, where once the L&N railroad hauled coal from the Jenkins, Blackey, and Eden Coal Companies.

Central to life in Blackey was the C. B. Caudill Store owned and operated by Joe Begley and Gaynell (Caudill) Begley. They sold dry goods, groceries, various tools, and had a sort of garage attached which also held car parts and supplies. The store served as a kind of gathering place for folks, much like the old hardware stores with the stoves and coffee cans

— Martha Carson —

Martha Carson **(1921–2004) was from Neon, Kentucky, in the eastern part of the state. Born Irene Amburgey, Carson was a glamorous, powerful country gospel singer who had a big hit with "Satisfied" (recorded by many but most lucratively by Elvis Presley). She also sang in a trio with her sisters Mattie and Minnie.**

Martha came on the tour once or twice as I remember, but the time I remember the most was the time she borrowed my guitar when her turn came to sing. I think it was our last show of the tour. When I got home, I took the guitar out to mess with it and heard a sound inside like a pick or string-end rattling around. I held the guitar over my head, shook it, and out came Martha Carson's fake fingernail which had fallen off while she was playing! I put it in my pick box and kept it for years until somehow, as small bits often do, it was gone. But the memory stays.

Dance at the Blackey, Kentucky, community center, 1968.

for "spittin' juice"—where politics were discussed, issues were raised, problems aired, and advice given. Joe Begley, who grew up in Kentucky, came back to live in Blackey when his wife Gaynell inherited her father's store.

In an oral history about the War on Poverty in Appalachia, Begley recounted his and his wife's involvement with what we would call social justice today. He "soon became involved with the Appalachian Volunteers (AVs) and other community activities including strip mining protests." Begley said the Caudill Store became a kind of nexus in Blackey, a "center for political discussion and an informal clearinghouse for information about how to get everything from legal help to medical services." Activists who passed through the store included Native peoples, Black Panthers, and folks like Myles Horton, who would go on to found the Highlander Research and Education Center. Begley was a true activist and community leader who later visited President Jimmy Carter in Washington to testify about issues plaguing Kentucky and Appalachia.

Ola Belle Reed

Ola Belle Reed (1916–2002), an old friend from the Sunset and New River Ranch music park days in the 1950s and ’60s, often came on the tour, sometimes with her husband, Bud. They both were great talkers and sitting between them in the van—Ola Belle talking in one ear and Bud in the other—was pretty drive-you-crazy great. Ola Belle was a songwriter, guitar and banjo player, and many of her songs speak of her life and traditions, and her sense of social justice. There was no one like her. She said what she meant and meant what she said. She claimed, all her life, much the same musical, guiding spirit, and moral territory as she had in the Sunset Park and New River Ranch days. She loved people, understood them, mentored many a musician, took in children who needed mothering and care, would give you the clothes off her back if she felt you needed them, and didn’t suffer fools gladly.

In 1986, Ola Belle was honored for her contributions to American folk music and culture with a National Heritage Fellowship. Manifested in her songwriting were the ideals that

she lived by: "Tear down the fences that fence us all in, fences created by such evil men" ("Tear Down the Fences"); "What we do for each other let us do it today . . . don't sing my praises after I'm gone" ("My Epitaph"); "High on the mountain standing all alone wondering where the years of my life have flown" ("High on a Mountain"); "I've worked for the rich, I've lived with the poor; I've seen many a heartache, there'll be many more, I've lived, loved and sorrowed, been to success's door. I've endured, I've endured, how long can one endure?" ("I've Endured")– are just a few of her countless and timeless lyrics that will endure forever.

FACING Always encouraging of young folks, Ola Belle Reed playing with some "young 'uns," as she would call them, at New River Ranch during a show, ca. 1956–57.

ABOVE (*Left to right*) David Reed, Ola Belle Reed, Mike Seeger, and Bud Reed at the Brandywine Mountain Music Convention, 1974.

The SFCRP tour often stopped in Blackey, Kentucky. Sometimes it was an overnight stay on the way to somewhere else, and sometimes we would put on a workshop or small concert. At that time, Joe Begley was involved in a big way with efforts to stop strip-mining and asked if we might do a small fundraiser in Blackey to turn out the community and help create solidarity. Joe and Gaynell were always glad to have us there and were the warmest of hosts. Often, there would be a dance or a workshop or small concert held in the old community center that, sadly, burned down sometime after 1979. Several scenes from the film *Coal Miner's Daughter*, with Sissy Spacek playing Loretta Lynn, were filmed around Blackey and in the Blackey community center.

My old friend Jack Wright, a Southwest Virginia activist and musician, wrote of his friend Joe, who died in 2000, "You know, Joe fought strip mining till the hour he died. He manned the phone at his bedside and continued organizing till the very end. What a wonderful human being. I miss him."

Band playing for the dance at the community center, Blackey, Kentucky, 1968. Everyone is having a good time.

We would sometimes take a break and stop to visit folks while on tour with the SFCRP. One of the memorable stops was a side trip to visit Peter and Polly Gott and family at their homestead in the rural mountains of Madison County, North Carolina. While there I took photos of our afternoon trek in the mountains near their home. Peter and Polly were originally from California and were among some of the first homesteaders dedicated to building everything from scratch, including their log cabin with no electricity at first, and a lovely doorless outhouse perched on the side of a hill near the cabin, with a beautiful view of the Western North Carolina mountains.

Another side trip was with the Blue Ridge Mountain Dancers, a group of young, energetic flatfoot dancers and precision cloggers from Hendersonville, North Carolina, headed up by husband and wife James and Arlene Kesterson. They would bring their own van along on tours and we'd convoy from gig to gig. They were always "deviling" each other, pranking and joking around. Once we passed them on a four-lane, I looked out the window to see Arlene and James switch places from passenger to driver's seat as they drove down the highway, laughing as our jaws hit the floor.

We were traveling from one gig to another in Eastern Kentucky (before roads were widened and to some degree straightened out); it was Halloween night and we were between towns. The roads were very winding, lots of hairpin turns, and the going was slow. As we carefully made our way, we could hear voices out among the trees laughing, and suddenly there was a tree across the road. We were trying to figure out what to do when a sheriff appeared behind us with a chainsaw, cut up the tree, and cleared the road. We continued on with the sheriff leading the way to remove any other logs we might encounter. He was nonplussed, as I remember. Par for the course in Eastern Kentucky on Halloween.

The couch in Tommy Jarrell's small living room was his favorite place for napping and playing music, 1978. Same for his huge dog, Bolliver.

Chapter 5

SPROUT WINGS AND FLY

I eat when I'm hungry, I drink when I'm dry
Get to feeling much better, I'm gonna sprout wings and fly.

—from "Drunken Hiccups" as sung and fiddled by Tommy Jarrell

Thomas Jefferson "Tommy" Jarrell (1901–85) was an old-time fiddler, singer, and banjo player who lived just outside of Mount Airy, North Carolina, in a community known as Toast—and yes, there was a Toast Coffeehouse. Tommy was the son of Benjamin Franklin "Ben" Jarrell, a member of DaCosta Woltz's Southern Broadcasters, who played and recorded some classic recordings in 1927. Tommy learned fiddle from his father and sounded remarkably like him.

FINDING TOMMY

Scott Odell, an expert on historical and traditional instruments, with a major interest in traditional music, remembers his first encounter with Tommy Jarrell this way: Sometime in the early 1960s Guthrie (Gus) Meade, a Kentucky scholar and documentarian of traditional music, suggested that Scott search for Ben Jarrell, the fiddler with DaCosta

Woltz's Southern Broadcasters. Scott found out Ben died in 1946 but that his son, Tommy, lived a short drive away. He found Tommy, and they had some talk and tunes. He returned a couple of days later with a Nagra tape recorder and drove Tommy to Low Gap to visit Tommy's old friend Fred Cockerham. Cockerham was a fine banjo and fiddle player who had often played with Tommy in the past but not in quite some time. Scott recorded Tommy and Fred playing four tunes, and later that summer he played the recordings for fellow old-time music enthusiast Rich Nevins. Nevins and Charlie Faurot (founder with Dave Freeman of County Records) were renting a house near Galax and were recording many of the old-timers. These recordings and many more, put out on County Records, became, as banjoist Tom Mylet noted, the cornerstone of the old-time music revival.

Traditional music was a pretty small world back then, and both Cece Conway, folklorist and author of *African Banjo Echoes in Appalachia*, and I got to know Tommy primarily through Alan Jabbour and Mike Seeger. We became friends and acolytes, spending many weeks with Tommy in 1976. Cece recorded Tommy for a radio show, taping many hours of him playing music, telling stories, and generally holding forth. I had twice applied for and received an NEA Apprenticeship Grant to study fiddle with him, and I spent a lot of time driving south from Washington, DC, to visit, and learn from Tommy, often accompanied by Mike.

We stayed with Tommy, and I kept something of a logbook during that time, between 1978 and 1980, keeping track of the tunes we worked on, the bowings, and other hints to help get at his distinctive and elusive fiddle style, and notes on his daily routines, his family, and his community. There were common themes in these notes, including alcoholism: his son, B. F., a generally nice person and good bluegrass fiddler who was also an alcoholic, was living with Tommy most of that time. There was often conflict between the two of them, partly due to what was perceived as B. F.'s resentment that his music was getting less attention than Tommy's, and partly due to the fact that B. F. could be unpleasant when he drank too much. You could say that Tommy was an alcoholic as well, but he had it much more under control.

Another theme throughout my logbook was how hard it was sometimes to spend time learning with Tommy, as neighbors and friends and family members were coming and going. One entry says, "Remember not to try to do lessons any time during the weekend. Too many people come by and Tommy can't ignore them and neither can we, [especially] when it's family and close friends. We got up at 10 today and practically immediately a brother of Mr. Tolbert dropped by—and seems to be staying on."

Music was always interspersed with conversation; religion, too. Tommy didn't go to church because, as he put it, "every church thinks they're the right one. What if I choose the wrong one!" He read the obituaries in the local paper every morning, keeping track of who had died, and, if it was someone he knew, he wanted to go to the viewing. Since Tommy didn't drive, we often took him. He once remarked that he wished "people would quit dying," as he was getting tired of having to go to so many funerals and viewings.

Eating and food was of course also a major accompaniment to everything. If we went to Corinna's or his daughter Ardena's or sisters Edith or Togie's house, it was corn, string beans, peas, chicken and dumplings or country fried steaks, potato salad, fried squash, cole slaw, banana pudding, peach or strawberry sonker. At Tommy's, it was potato soup (a kettle of water into which you put cut-up potatoes, a whole lot of margarine, and salt), pork fat, and pinto beans. A constant irritant for Tommy was his inability to get the right kind of buckwheat flour to make the pancakes that he loved and remembered. We found a

Tommy's living room in Toast, North Carolina, 1978. (*Left to right*) Tommy, Mike Seeger, and Tommy's two sons, Benjamin Franklin "BF" Jarrell and Wayne Jarrell.

package at a mill one time and brought it to him. He made the buckwheat pancake batter, which had to sit for at least twenty-four hours. Woke up the next morning to find that the batter had overflowed the bowl and was all over the kitchen floor; apparently, he had put in too much yeast. He was obsessive about getting the pancakes just right. It took him a while, but he finally succeeded in getting a good batch, which he served with "streaky gravy" made by pouring coffee into leftover fat and leavings.

He'd make the coffee at the beginning of the week in a large aluminum percolator, then perc and reperc it throughout the week until it was practically mud. When Les Blank was on site, we would note to Tommy that Les was from California and wanted his special Peet's coffee that he had brought along, which we also drank happily!

A stay with Tommy involved entering into his family and community life that included visits to friends he wanted to see, the old homeplace and family graveyard, community events like dances, or some local event where Tommy would play music and where we'd often accompany him.

Tommy loved animals. He had a big—at least hundred-pound—rangy black stray dog that wandered into his yard. Tommy named him Bolliver ("After that there dictator Simon Bolliver") and before long Bolliver was Tommy's beloved buddy. A squirrel family lived in a tree outside Tommy's kitchen, and he would go out with peanuts. He'd chirp "Here squirrely, here squirrely, come on squirrely," in a high little voice, trying to get them to eat out of his hand.

On every few pages in my notes there are receipts—I was accountable to the NEA since the apprenticeship grant money primarily went to the artist, with a little toward my expenses. In my handwriting is "Received from Alice Gerrard $200 for fiddle lessons," then his signature, "Thomas Jefferson Jarrell," and the date. Often Mike was with me, and we would stay for several days or a week at a time. When we would leave to go home, it was always a little sad. We hated to leave, and Tommy hated to see us go. We overheard Tommy saying his prayers one night before we left to go home: "God bless Mike and Alice on their way home."

Mike and I traveled a fair amount with Tommy, taking his music all through the United States and Canada on traditional music tours hosted by colleges, festivals, folklore societies, organized by Mike and bookers of traditional music like John Ullmann of Portland, Oregon. As I remember, the first one of these tours involved flying, something Tommy had never done. He was a little bit worried but also wanted to go, and his family was very worried about him, so there was some convincing needed and assurances that he'd be taken care of. It all worked out and Tommy ended up a seasoned traveler. He always woke up pretty early, and often during a tour I'd hear him knocking on various of our motel doors: "Hey, you fellers gonna sleep all day?" He, of course, would be fully dressed in his suit and tie and hat and had probably been sitting around since six o'clock waiting.

FILMS AND FOOD

Sometime in 1977, Cece Conway came to me with a proposition. She wanted to make a film about Tommy capturing full performances of his tunes and songs and an exploration of the connection between Tommy's music and that of traditional African American musicians, as well as his relationship to his community and the role it played in his music. Tommy had pointed out that when guitars came into the area in the early 1900s, Black people and women were the first to play them. There were two songs in particular that he played and credited to African Americans. One was the magnificent "Boll Weevil," which he learned from a Black woman who was singing the song at a tent show he snuck into as a teenager; the other, "Raleigh and Spencer" he remembered hearing often from a neighbor, Jim Raleigh, who would walk down the road past young Tommy's house playing his guitar and singing the song as he walked on. By the time we got to work on the film, Jim Raleigh had died, but we had a nice visit with his wife and children who still lived up the road.

Cece's plan was that I would be the music consultant, Les Blank (filmmaker of such gems as *The Blues Accordin' to Lightnin' Hopkins*, *A Well Spent Life* about Mance Lipscomb, *Werner Herzog Eats His Shoe*, and many more) the cinematographer, and Mike Seeger the sound technician. Mike and I jumped at the chance. Cece wrote the grant to the NEA, and Les was willing. All we needed to do was convince Tommy that this was a good idea.

As anyone who's ever written a grant knows, you need support letters from respected people in the field in which you are working, as well as a letter from your subject agreeing to the whole shebang. I wrote Tommy a letter, basically outlining what we hoped to accomplish with the film project, the time frame, the finances, and why we felt such a project was important. This was his response:

TOP Getting ready to film, ca. 1978. (*Left to right*) Scotty East, guitarist and singer; Les Blank, with camera; Chester McMillian, guitar player; Tommy; Earnest East, a fiddler who headed up Earnest East's Pine Ridge Boys & Patsy, a well-known local band; and Mike Seeger, with sound equipment.

BOTTOM Surry County, North Carolina, 1978. During the filming of *Sprout Wings and Fly*, Tommy's sister Togie and her husband Joe hosted a picnic for all of us. It was set up on the picnic table in their yard. We feasted on steaks, potato salad and other salads, beans, and of course Corinna's peach sonker, the highlight of the desserts. Tommy's older sister Julie Lyons (*standing at left*), loved to play the harmonica and sing songs and ballads, and she was known for her flatfoot dancing. At the time of our filming she was seventy-six. There is a short film that came from footage of *Sprout Wings and Fly* called *Julie: Old Time Tales of the Blue Ridge*. Also pictured, seated at the table (*left to right*), are Ardena Moncus, Tommy's daughter; Tommy; Cece Conway; and Corinna Bowden, Tommy's special lady friend.

> Hello. I have been studying about the movie ever since I got your letter. I have decided I will help you all make the movie. If there is no commercial TV. You know how I feel about commercial TV. They will have to set the money bags down to me if they want a commercial TV. Give Cece a wee bit of a hug for me when you see her. I am looking forward to seeing you all soon. Come on down soon as you can and we will talk a lot, fiddle some, drink a little, have a hell of a good time. Eat some chicken and dumplings along with some potato soup, ha ha.
>
> By for now. I love you all a whole lot—Tommy.

He usually signed his letters Thomas Jefferson Jarrell (Tommy) with a circle around the "Tommy."

We received supportive letters from Dan Patterson, at that time professor of English and folklore at UNC, and Dewey Balfa, Cajun fiddler and singer from Basile, Louisiana, who was invested in keeping his own local music culture thriving. In addition, Les Blank wrote a support letter agreeing to use all his camera, recording, and editing equipment as an in-kind contribution.

We were thrilled when we got the grant, and at various times between 1978 and 1983 we filmed, recorded, and edited more than twenty hours of footage, which we edited into the half-hour film *Sprout Wings and Fly*. We all basically moved in with Tommy in his small house. Mike and I got the spare bedroom; Cece got one couch and Les the other. There were fine times, hard times, disagreements, agreements, eating, drinking, and great music and stories.

Occasionally Tommy's daughter Ardena would come over and cook a feast of chicken and dumplings and biscuits, or we would go to his friend Corinna's home and she'd serve up a fine country meal with plenty of vegetables and peach sonker (a local term for cobbler). Corinna Bowden was a special friend of Tommy's, a woman likely in her early seventies, who shared Tommy's love of bluegrass festivals, especially if Bill Monroe and Kenny Baker were going to be there. She would drive him, and they hung out together often. In the film, their friendship came up with a question about whether they had ever talked about getting married. With one voice they said they had talked about it but decided against it. Corinna spoke up with something to the effect of "Why would I want to get married? I can do what I want, pack up my little gritchel [combination of satchel and grip], go when I want, come back when I want and no one to say I can't." I'm sure she spoke for many women, married or unmarried.

When we filmed a sequence at his sister Togie's home, there was always a feast—a banquet of steaks on the grill along with many tasty side dishes. One time Les (a good cook as well as filmmaker) cooked up some delicious fried chicken in a wonderful batter that contained a little hot pepper. Most of the time it was potatoes, beans, and fat meat with Tommy—I'm not complaining, mind you, I love all that stuff—but it did get a little boring. We were delighted when one day Stu Cohen, owner of a vintage musical instrument store near Boston, pulled his camper up in Tommy's yard completely equipped with a gourmet kitchen and all the condiments for Chinese cooking. He and his wife Deane proceeded to cook up a fantastic Chinese meal and we sat around eating in Tommy's yard. Tommy thrived on the sameness of his diet and wasn't one to experiment with new tastes; he gingerly tried a few things, but mostly they weren't his cup of tea. We, however, were thrilled.

There is one Tommy and food story that I can still picture clearly: Andy Cahan, Tommy, and I were performing at the 1982 World's Fair in Knoxville, Tennessee. Andy and I decided to go to a Chinese restaurant for supper one night. Tommy gamely said he'd go with us, and we hoped we'd find something he would eat. We went pretty early, maybe around 4, and there were only the three of us and a waiter in the restaurant. I looked at a menu trying to suss out what might appeal to Tommy. It appeared he might like dumplings, so we ordered and when the food came, Tommy just stared at his dumplings for a while. Then he looked over at the waiter who was standing by the kitchen door and motioned him over, saying, "Hey buddy, hey could you come over here a minute?" The waiter came to the table and Tommy said, "Hey buddy, do you have any light bread?" I had to explain to the waiter that this meant white bread. No, they didn't have any, but he'd be happy to go out and get some for Tommy. He came back with a loaf, put it on our table; Tommy opened it up, took out a slice and happily proceeded to sop up the duck sauce with the bread, thus surviving his second encounter with Chinese food.

THE CAMERAS ROLL ON

My and Cece's general modus operandi on a working day was to get up in the morning and drive to nearby Dobson for coffee to review what we had accomplished the day before and what needed to be done that day. We'd also buy Tommy's favorite, I. W. Harper 101-proof bourbon, and sometimes flowers for relatives and neighbors. We strategized, plotted, planned, working around possible hurt feelings, demands for attention, the needs of the film, and the needs of family and community, which sometimes didn't coincide. It was intense.

There were many wonderful, awful, funny, and dramatic stories from those weeks we spent. One took place at banjo player Dix Freeman's old home place, where we were planning on filming a home dance in the old style. We planned to clear out a room or maybe two and have the musicians in the doorway playing for the dancers. Dix presented our cinematographer Les with a mason jar of white liquor—commonly known as moonshine. Dix brought down the moonshine from its hiding place in the woods and set it down in front of Les, challenging him to a drinking contest. It must be mentioned that Les was very stoic and poker-faced in demeanor, rarely giving a clue as to his state of mind, which kind of drove Dix crazy.

Tommy took the jar, shook it, announcing to Les that the more beads that formed and the longer they took to settle, the better the liquor. Dix set the jar down between them on the floor, Les took a sip, Dix took a sip, Les took a sip. . . . This went on until Dix was thoroughly soused and Les was calm and inscrutable as usual. The whole shebang culminated in Dix's announcement to us all that he was going to do something he had always wanted to do: pee in his wife Charlie's sink. Fortunately, Charlie walked in, heard him, and grabbed him before he could execute the deed. She was mad as hell and Dix spent a lot of time the next day apologizing to all and sundry for his lapse of good taste.

Somewhere during the filming, we were talking with Paul Sutphin, a wonderful guitar player and singer from Mount Airy. He was the guitar player of choice for two well-known string bands in the area: the Smokey Valley Boys and the Camp Creek Boys. I can picture him: he geared up, tilted his chair back, chuckled a bit, and proceeded to tell us about his dream that he was walking barefoot on a "field of titties." He had such a wry sense of humor and told it with a twinkle in his eye and his signature gap-toothed smile. Somehow that scene didn't get into the film.

We felt it was an important part of our mandate to include the community and get feedback as filming progressed, so we showed a ninety-minute edit of *Sprout Wings and Fly* at the Surry Community College. We invited family, friends, and community to attend, and held a Q&A after the showing. Folks loved the footage—especially the nature scenes, and there was general approval of the film.

The raw footage is currently in the Southern Folklife Collection. Harrod Blank (Les's son) and Cece have been avidly applying for funds so it can be digitized for future generations. It would be wonderful if this could happen, making the footage available to watch, use for research, and generally access.

The filming and editing of *Sprout Wings and Fly* took us a long time with all the various schedules, but what a reward when, after the world premiere in Chapel Hill, our big Mount Airy premiere at the Andy Griffith Playhouse took place on November 3, 1984. I went around putting flyers on car windshields, in parking lots at various factories—just all over the place. With Rachel Smith's help, we convinced the mayor to declare November 3 "Tommy Jarrell Day." Rachel was a supporter of the arts and the president of the Surry Arts Council board of directors. She was a close friend of Mount Airy native son Andy Griffith and his mother and had many useful contacts in town. She offered us her help, and rounded up the "high muck-a-mucks" (as Elizabeth Cotten used to call the upper crust) of Mount Airy, and got Dr. Dale Simmons, a supporter of the arts, to host a big dinner at his home for Tommy and his family, the filmmakers, and various local musicians who were set to play at the showing of the film.

My old friend Ralph Rinzler, who was director of the Office of Folklife Programs at the Smithsonian Institution and founding director of the Festival of American Folklife, came to the premiere. After his return to Washington, Ralph sent a copy of the following letter that he had written to Alan Jabbour, director of the American Folklife Center at the Library of Congress, who was unable to attend:

> Here is a brief report on Tommy Jarrell Day in Mt. Airy, NC, last Saturday. . . . The afternoon session was well attended but not sold out. It had the feeling of an all-in-the-family rehearsal with many small details going awry and no one minding a bit. Applause was generous—everyone there was local and proud of Mt. Airy's "favorite son."
>
> A local physician gave a large dinner reception for Tommy, his family and friends. The evening concert was back at the theater. . . . The crowd was huge and very warm. Everyone was up for something special, and they got it.
>
> Tommy had a hip flask which he used very discreetly. He sparkled and played like a demon cracking jokes and looking mischievous. The high point was a set of banjo/fiddle duets in which Tommy and an 83-year-old woman banjo picker [Bertie Mae Dickens] played tunes they had not played together since the 20s. They were both masters of their instruments and displayed a noble, proud image which commanded a standing ovation twice

Gerrard & Conway
with
The Surry Arts Council
present

Sprout Wings & Fly

A Portrait of North Carolina Fiddler
Tommy Jarrell

*"I'll tune up my fiddle, I'll rosin my bow
I'll make myself welcome wherever I go.
I'll eat when I'm hungry, I'll drink when I'm dry
If I get to feeling much better,
I'll sprout wings and fly."*
. . . learned from Houston Galyean

The "Sprout Wings and Fly" Show
Andy Griffith Playhouse
November 3, 1984

LEFT The program that we handed out at the film.

BOTTOM Galax, Virginia, 1984. Tommy Jarrell, with fiddle, and Bertie Mae Dickens, with banjo, playing together at a cookout I had at my home. Behind them watching are musician Mac Traynham (*standing*) and guitarist Chester McMillian (*seated*).

during their performance. It was like something you might have seen and heard half a century ago—like one of Alan Lomax's field recordings come to life. The visual impact as well as the music itself overwhelmed everyone.

Cece Conway read the Endowment and Folklife Center letters proudly at each performance; they added a welcome and important dimension. The film is excellent and received the community's approval. Someone commented that it was interesting to note where the community audience laughed spontaneously at points which elicited no response from outsiders who had seen the film.

Following the evening performance, a huge crowd gathered at Tommy's house for country ham, biscuits, cake and cider. Tommy also had a few full fruit jars [of white liquor] and that fuel kept the two or three multi-fiddle string bands going at full tilt until 5 am. Tommy was ahead of it all throughout the night, moving from one group to another, joining in with his fiddle, a joke or two and an offer of another swig. It would have fueled your soul for a good time to come. . . .

Warm regards,
Ralph

There was indeed a huge party at Tommy's after the showing. My children came down for the event; friends came from near and far. The house was overflowing with music and people indoors and out, dancing wherever there were a couple of feet of floor space. It felt wonderful, but best of all Tommy loved it and was bursting with pride. A glorious night to remember.

It seemed like he'd live forever, but about a year later in January 1985, Tommy was gone, surely making the heavens ring, playing music with his old friend Charlie Lowe, with a gaggle of others waiting their turn, taking a snort, and telling stories.

Chapter 6

A LIFETIME IN LESS THAN A DECADE

I feel that one of the great life gifts I was given was the opportunity to live among some of the greatest traditional musicians of all time. From 1981 to 1989, when I lived just outside the little town of Galax in Southwest Virginia, several older players were still around; those who played in the old, lilting style of noting and bowing that helped define the early fiddle sound that prevailed in the Galax region. I chose to live in this community and was actively involved. I did not pursue my taping and photographing, at first, with a project in mind. But I somehow knew that these were great moments in time and that it was important to record them. Perhaps this is the true spirit of the documentarian, I don't know, but that's what I did.

In 1980, after my ten-year marriage to Mike Seeger ended in divorce, I was eager to get away from suburban Maryland. We sold the house. My son Joel was working and living on his own; my youngest son Jesse, who had just graduated from high school, moved in with Joel.

The two girls were in college. I decided to move to Nashville and figure out what my next steps would be. I had some idea of writing songs, trudging around to publishers, and getting into the "music biz."

When I think back on that time, I marvel that Mike and I were so absorbed in our own problems and needs that we just up and left the kids on their own. I carry a lot of guilt for that. I think of other friends of mine, women with children, who wanted to carve out a path for themselves in difficult circumstances. I think particularly of Rosalie Sorrels, the wonderful singer, storyteller, and songwriter who was left with five children and no financial support after her divorce. She chose her musical path and carried around a lot of guilt, her choices being between dragging five children along on the road with her or staying home with the kids and not doing what she loved. I think a lot of women experience this scenario in one form or another. You live on your own, you want to do your thing, don't have much money or emotional support, can't afford a nanny, don't have family around to help out, etc. Rosalie's was a lifelong condition, mine was only temporary, but still there are family scars.

A sign in the window of a store in downtown Galax, 1984.

Side street in downtown Galax, 1984.

My son Jesse put it very aptly when he said, "I think we're all still recovering from those times." My daughter Jenny, who was around nineteen or twenty at the time, recalled that she felt as though she had to be the mother to Jesse and Joel, who were struggling to adapt to this new reality that they were facing. Jesse notes that it wasn't until much later that he realized how fucked up that situation really was.

After I got to Nashville, I stayed with my friend Anne Romaine, from the Southern Folk Cultural Revival Project, who rented me the small outbuilding in her backyard on Valeria Street. (Kirk McGee of Sam and Kirk McGee, early Grand Ole Opry stars, lived in the house behind Anne.) I spent many hours playing the guitar and writing, hanging out with Anne, who was also divorced, and her small daughter Rita.

I loved country music but the days when you could turn the radio dial and immediately recognize which one was the country station were disappearing. The country music played on the radio at that time had started the gradual decline into sounding like watered-down pop music. By living in Nashville, I was missing the older, more traditional sounds of country music—the not-so-perfect, gritty edginess, soul sounds without strings, that were becoming less valued in the country music business as it strove to become more middle class, more mainstream, more "crossover," less root-bound.

Two young, talented musician friends of mine, Paul Brown and Andy Cahan, originally from New York, were also very drawn to Southwest Virginia and its historical musical importance as well as its currently active music community. They had moved to Galax in order to live "in" the music. Over some time and a number of conversations, I grew to feel that if I wanted to learn the music, I should do the same—go to the source of what turned out to be the last hurrah, the last deep breath of the classic old-time music as played by elders who mostly learned it from their parents and neighbors in their communities, before the advent of records and radios. So, around 1981, I moved to Galax, Virginia. The Fiddlers Convention fairgrounds were situated about two miles from my house.

At that time, Galax was a small industrial town based around the furniture factory and various hosiery mills. Downtown there were local little businesses, a hardware store, churches, a bank, a couple of secondhand stores, an old Baptist church turned into the Rooftop of Virginia, a Community Action Program where one could buy traditional quilts, homemade knives, wood carvings, and a host of other items made by local people; there was a movie theater, a couple of cafés, a Hardee's, a dingy motel on Main Street. Ronald Reagan's "trickle down" economic policies held that if you lowered taxes for the rich and for corporations, the money they would save would trickle down to poorer people and even things out. Well, that wasn't happening in Galax or any other town in Southwest Virginia, so far as I could see.

On the outskirts of town, things were changing a bit as Interstate 77 edged through the area to meet Interstate 81. A Western Steer restaurant opened up (exotic because of the salad bar), as well as McDonald's and Arby's. A modern movie theater opened just outside of town, and there was the usual array of strip mall scenery.

FINDING THE FOLK

Nowadays you can learn traditional music and crafts at music "camps" or workshops or schools that have sprung up throughout the country and overseas, where musicians are hired to teach their particular expertise: fiddle, banjo, singing, songwriting, basket making, etc. Students attend the camps for usually a week, taking classes and participating in jam sessions and performances, having a big time and making (often lasting) friends. Mostly middle-class, mostly white (although that is changing gradually as more and more young African Americans are reclaiming their rightful heritage in traditional music), mostly of similar backgrounds, they spend the week happily immersed in music or dance or crafts.

Choosing to live in a community, most likely very different from what you're used to, is more complicated. The food, the language or dialects, accents, the rhythms of speech, the subtleties of behavior, cultural differences; learning to hold back, listen, and learn. I learned that it was okay to badmouth someone if you did it in a certain way—that is, "He's kind of like me, ain't got no sense." And if the host says "stay with us" at the end of a visit it doesn't mean that you should stay. It's just a formality, as a friend learned the hard way when he jumped back out of the car and went back into the house, prepared to spend the night—awkward! And when people urge more food on you at the table, as they always do, and you're stuffed to the gills, it's okay to refuse if you say, "I don't believe I will." Running into someone on the street may involve a conversation that's hard to get out of with lots of "well . . . well . . . wells" and ultimately, "Well, I'll let you go." You can't rush things. Once a musician friend from "up north" in Maryland was visiting and we went to visit a local fiddler and play some music. Typically these sessions involve playing a tune, talking a little or a lot until someone says, "Well, what do you want to play?" "Well, I don't care, whatever you want." "Well, I don't care neither," until somehow consensus emerges and off you go into another tune. This drove my friend nuts and prompted her to say very abruptly, "Will someone please make up their minds?!"

I was fortunate to know Tommy Jarrell, who lived "down the mountain" about twenty minutes from Galax. My friends Paul and Andy had broken some ground for me in and around town, so fortunately I wasn't going stone cold into a situation where I knew nobody.

I was going to need a place to live. Paul Brown had introduced me to Luther Davis, an old fiddler and farmer who lived just outside of Galax.

Luther knew a local state trooper, a Mr. Barton, who had a four-room house for rent at fifty dollars a month, and about a mile and a half from Luther's home. It was set back off the road accessible by a long, rutty, tree-lined driveway that opened out into a field—the red, tar paper–covered little shack sitting alone in the middle surrounded by tall grass. The house had running water pumped from a spring and an indoor bathroom with a big old clawfoot bathtub. I moved in my Ashley Wood stove, got a cheap secondhand refrigerator, a cord of wood, and I was set.

Becoming compatriots in our musical odyssey, Andy Cahan and I spent as much time as possible visiting older musicians, people who could tell us what it was like in the old days, what the music was like, what life was like. Although in their late seventies, eighties, and nineties, many of these musicians continued to play, albeit infrequently and often with a nod to aging memories, fingers that didn't work so well anymore, and arms that moved more slowly. We always took our instruments with us on our forays in case they might remember a tune or song that we could learn. Hearing us play often encouraged them to pick up their fiddle or banjo—something they might not have done in a long while. We looked into local history, tracked down friends and relatives of musicians, and asked questions. They enjoyed having us come around and stir up old memories and music. As ninety-plus-year-old Luther once put it, "If you'd all come once in a while, you'd all sort of keep me alive."

At some point along the way, we applied for and received a Virginia Arts Council grant (as well as many private contributions) to help put out a recording and booklet project, *The Old-Time Way*, documenting three musician friends with unusual repertoires and direct connections to an old way of life and a strong musical tradition: Luther Davis, Roscoe, and Leone Parish. Fiddler player Luther Franklin Davis (1887–1986) was probably the person I visited most often—his home was only a couple of miles from mine. His wife Alverda had died long ago, and he lived by himself in the farmhouse that had been his married home and where he and Alverda had raised their daughters "Billy" and "Jack" (actually, Ruth and Mary) and their son Kyle. Luther was a very lean, very tall man, with his height cut almost in half in his old age by a severe stoop so that he was pretty much L-shaped most of the time he was standing. A thin wispy cap of white hair covered his narrow head; he was sharp-featured with bright, knowing eyes behind round steel-rimmed glasses, and he always had a thin stain of tobacco juice that ran in the crease from the corners of his mouth down to his chin. (After Luther died, an old friend of his who was at the funeral parlor

Luther Davis, 1984.

viewing, commented, "He sure looks natural but he'd look more natural if he had a little stream of tobacco juice running down his chin.")

Luther was a charismatic man with a powerful personality, and as long as he lived, he planted a large vegetable garden each spring, harvesting and canning the vegetables that he raised. He cooked his own meals, made his own biscuits—all on a wood stove. Although he had an electric stove, I don't recall him ever using it. He didn't like it, in the same way he refused to set his clocks to daylight savings time. He was frugal, with a strong sense of right and wrong, fairness, and his own place in time. Besides farming, Luther had been a deputy sheriff and auctioneer, traveling around the countryside a great deal, selling at auction livestock, property, and household goods.

Luther had many stories to tell about the old days, and with his sharp mind and prodigious memory, he brought them to life while I soaked it all up. He talked a lot about his special mentors, Isom (1856–1926) and Fielden (1857–1929) Rector, two brothers living nearby from whom Luther learned many of his tunes when he was growing up. Isom lived with his family in one end of a long log house, while Fielden lived at the other end with his family.

Andy worked in a woodworking shop in Independence, Virginia, and often brought Luther wood for his cookstove—pieces of cherry, maple, walnut, and ash. Luther loved to whittle, and often the wood meant for burning went to his pocketknife. When we'd go to visit, he'd often be sitting on his enclosed porch whittling away on some little something—a small, old-time pitchfork so we would know what one looked like, a sweet little carved wooden box containing banjo bridges with "LFD 1984" written on them, a spoon, and a couple of fiddle bridges. Treasures.

He told us about being a little boy of maybe seven and seeing his grandfather, a Civil War veteran, gathered with other old soldiers and racing their horses across the fields, jumping fences, with their long, white beards flowing out behind them.

"Oh, I was scared to death," Luther said. I could just see those old men, the horses galloping, and the scared but fascinated child. Another time, Luther recalled a neighbor stopping by the house after supper to let Luther's father know that some strangers were in the barn. His father went to investigate and brought back with him two Italians—one with a bagpipe-like instrument, one with a small barrel organ—and a monkey (Luther remembered being scared of the monkey). His father called neighbors on the old crank-handle phone to come over, and soon a musical evening ensued with bagpipe music and a dancing monkey.

THE PAST COMES TO LIFE

Luther, who had lived through the invention of the automobile, radio, airplane, TV, and the moon landing, would often say he found life lonely. There were few his age around anymore who had lived through the same things he had, but he loved talking to his younger visitors, telling of his life, letting us know who he was, and talking about his friends and mentors. If there is consolation in being in your nineties, becoming more and more aware that your time is short, I imagine that much of it comes from telling your story. If he told us his story and played us his music, we would do the same as we went through life and thus, his legacy would be passed on down through the generations.

And it's true, that when you go to an old-time music festival, fiddlers convention, or old-time music gathering pretty much anywhere in the country and maybe the world you are likely to hear fragments of Luther's tunes wafting through the campground—"Lily of the Valley," "Flying Indian Waltz," "I Walked That Pretty Girl Home," "West

Luther Davis imparting wisdom to his visitors, Rusty Neithammer and Nancy Dols Neithammer, 1983.

Virginia Farewell," and so many more. Luther talked a lot about an old-time fiddler from Sweden, Magnus Norman, who came to visit him often during the Fiddlers Convention, which Magnus attended for a few years. I met Magnus years later when I toured Sweden with Tom Sauber and Brad Leftwich, and he remembered Luther with great fondness.

Luther and others often commented on their age, conscious that they were forgetting things and not playing as well as they used to. Parley Parsons, an old fiddler friend of Luther's said, "I used to run my counter [old term for a fiddle bass string] up. I just got tired of changing my fiddle I reckon. . . . I know 100 tunes if I can just think of them. You know, old age you get so your mind don't work just right. Sometimes I'll sit down to play, and I can't even think of a tune, and I'll just put my fiddle up."

Luther also had a wry sense of humor, and I noted in a scrapbook that is now in the Southern Folklife Collection, a rhyme he once recited:

> *Colonel, your sporting days are over,*
> *Your parking light is out*
> *What used to be your joy pole*
> *Is now your water spout.*

Luther knew where his tunes came from, who he had learned them from, and always talked about his mentors. "'West Virginia Farewell' come from West Virginia, from Marshall Smith," he told me. "He went to West Virginia and got him a job on a section force. . . . He got killed there; fell off a trestle." Luther was a fine singer, and he learned the song "Lonesome Dove" from May Lyons. "She was a banjo picker. I knowed the family for some time but I was runnin' a threshin' machine at that time and we was threshin' for her father and had to stay a whole night. . . . We all got to playin' there that night and May jumped onto that ["Lonesome Dove"] and I never had heard it before, but I learned it right there from May and I thought it was beautiful. That must've been about 1903 or '04." He often played tunes in honor of his mentors: "["Stay All Night"] is 'Uncle' Isom's tune. He thought so much of it. Not much of a tune but I'm a-goin' to play it."

He played a beautiful tune, "Pineywoods Girl of Virginia," that he learned from Friel Lowe, who probably learned it from legendary local fiddler Greenberry ("Green") Leonard (ca. 1810–92). Most musical communities have their legendary musician from the past—the one who is referred to in conversations—"I learned this tune from my father, and he learned it from his father, who learned it from [legendary musician].” Anyone who knew Leonard personally was long dead, although almost every old musician I encountered in and around Galax mentioned him and retold tales about his prowess. Since he was never recorded of course, there are only clues to Green Leonard’s fiddle style; we never found any photographs of him, but even tracing a tune back to him was exciting. We have clues to Leonard’s playing because another local fiddle legend, Emmett Lundy (1864–1953), who was recorded by the Lomaxes in the 1940s, had apparently learned a lot of his repertoire from Leonard.

Luther told me of walking twelve miles when he was sixteen to learn “Pineywoods Girl” from Friel Lowe. “We didn’t have tape recorders, but we didn’t play it just once, we played a half a dozen times the night before, and we played it again the next morning. Lord, I was young then, and [my head] had plenty of room; and when I left there I could play ‘Pineywoods Girl.’”

I found that sometimes the children of these musician elders like Luther viewed things a little differently than their parents’ younger visitors did. While their children loved their mothers and fathers and were always there for them, they were often less interested in their parents’ artistic, folkloric, or historical legacies. They primarily wanted to make sure their parents were well taken care of, and that they not do anything that would keep them from getting into the *good* afterlife. In a community where getting by was not easy a lot of the time, these children or grandchildren addressed the day-to-day family worries and concerns

Sept. 28, 1984
"Fellows like Luther
avis & Ben & Charlie
arrell & them Edmonds &
Wade Ward & Charlie
Higgins & Charlie Lowe,
are the ones that preserved
that old time music around
there, & it would have
been gone if it hadn't of it
been for them a-keepin'
goin'. Fellows like him
& Zack Payne & Pat
McKinney & Emmett Lundy
was the backbone of that
old time music. Old man
Luther Davis ought to have
one of them awards. And
that's the way I feel
about it."
Thomas J Jarrell (Tommy)

Tommy’s letter in support of Luther Davis. He dictated it to me and then signed it with his usual addition of “Tommy” with a circle around it.

that we didn't have. We were able to give ourselves completely to the project at hand—listening, learning, recording, photographing. In the case of Luther, not having anyone living at home with him, he was free to pursue his interests as he wanted.

A local African American woman, Mabel Crockett, was hired by his family to come in and cook and clean for Luther during a period of time when he couldn't get around too well. Mable encouraged Luther to play his music and he encouraged her to sing. She called him "Brother Luther," and I'll never forget the time when they tried to make some music together. Luther tried to play a hymn, accompanying Mable, who had a great voice and was a fine singer. It didn't work out too well (Luther was in one key and Mabel in another for starters), and I have the cassette tapes to prove it—but that didn't matter. They kept going and they got along fine and enjoyed themselves.

At the end of a visit as I would get ready to leave, Luther would often pull a little guilt trip out of his repertoire: "I've known people who said they'd come back, and they didn't, and then the person died, and they were sorry."

Andy and I nominated Luther for an NEA Heritage Award in 1984 (he didn't receive one), but we were thrilled that Tommy Jarrell wrote a letter in 1984 in support of our nomination (shown on previous page).

Nancy (Dols) Neithammer, a young woman originally from California, had come to the Southeast specifically to try and learn Tommy Jarrell's fiddle style. She got a job in Winston-Salem and lived there, traveling back and forth to Mount Airy to spend time with Tommy, learning his style of playing. She became a wonderful player and got as close to Tommy's style as anyone I can think of. During her several years living in the area, she also became friends with Luther.

As most fiddlers know, it's all about the bowing, and someone came up with the idea to make a video that would show fiddle bowing patterns if a light were attached to the fiddler's wrist. Then they would be filmed in the dark so the lights would show up the bowing patterns. Banjoist Rusty Neithammer devised a way to attach a light to the wrist, Surry Community College donated some old black-and-white analog equipment, and they went to the college and filmed Tommy in a dark room so that the light patterns showed the movement of Tommy's bow beautifully. It's pretty amazing stuff. Luther was less patient with the process, so they only got a little of him, but Paul Brown made a wonderful film of Luther at home—going about his daily routine and playing music a little. These videos are in the Southern Folklife Collection at UNC.

Brother and sister Roscoe and Leone Parish, 1984. They often played songs together—Roscoe on fiddle or banjo and Leone holding down the pump organ or guitar.

The other two musicians on *The Old-Time Way* recording project were Roscoe (1897–1984) and Leone Parish (1902–88), brother and sister, who lived on a beautiful large farm in Carroll County, Virginia. The Parish homeplace was near the Coal Creek Community in the rolling farmland just below Fisher's Peak, where North Carolina and Virginia meet. Roscoe was a banjo and fiddle player, and Leone (known as "Miss Lyn") played guitar and pump organ and sang. They lived in adjacent houses, Leone in the old family-built home where they had grown up, and Roscoe and his wife Arizona (called Zona, pronounced "Zoney") in the house they had built next to the old family home. You could step out of one house, walk a few steps and be at the other's back door.

By the time we met the Parishes, Roscoe had developed dementia that severely affected his memory. Still, he knew a range of rare and wonderful tunes as well as a lot of popular-type ones—he particularly liked "Pop Goes the Weasel." "Have I played 'Pop Goes the Weasel' for you?" he would often say, forgetting he had just played it. He didn't always remember the names of tunes, but he never forgot the tunes themselves and often whom he learned them from—mostly his father and sometimes others in the community.

Leone Parish, Carroll County, Virginia, 1987.

Roscoe was soft-spoken, gentle, and had many talents. He built his own banjo complete with a cow-bone bridge that gave it a beautiful bell-like sound; he had been a semiprofessional photographer and was, in general, a fine craftsman. Leone was dignified and well spoken—good behavior, manners, and traditions meant a lot to her. She knitted, crocheted, tatted, painted, and loved to read. She told me she was named after a "musical and artistic" girl in a novel her mother had read just before she was born, "so Mother wished that [name] on me." Roscoe and Leone both read music, and in addition to the tunes Roscoe had learned from his father and other folks in the community, he had a copy of *One Thousand Fiddle Tunes*, printed by M. M. Cole Publishing, and enjoyed playing a few hornpipes he'd learned from it. The Parishes were always welcoming and glad to see us coming.

Roscoe often talked about how music was a healing art, and how when he was a child and had been sick for a long time, the doctor prescribed learning the banjo. Roscoe always felt that music helped to heal him, and I believe it did. He once said, "If you get down with the blues, you're sick all over before you know it. But if you play the fiddle or banjo and you enjoy it, you never get blue. And it'll rest you more than anything. My daddy always said the best sleep he ever got was to let us go on and make music and for him to go to sleep—that done him more good than anything. Well, you can believe it—it's not hard to believe. It'll rest you to a certain extent. It'll just make you feel a little better to have music about you. . . . Pleasant thoughts . . . help you." Gentle and loving people, I will never forget them.

There were many other local musicians we spent time with that weren't included in Andy's and my recording project, but whom we recorded and photographed and to whom we are forever grateful. At some point, Andy and I had the idea to try and get as many of the old-generation musicians together in one place as we could. That place was my field, where we organized a cookout. It was a beautiful day, and people started arriving in the early afternoon, parked their cars, got out their chairs, their instruments, and their contributions to the food. Almost as soon as folks arrived, the music started. It was a meeting of musical giants: Tommy Jarrell, Luther Davis, Ernest East, Whit Sizemore, John Rector, John Patterson, Bertie Mae Dickens, and Faye Wagoner, just to name a few. The younger and middle generations were there, too: Dale Morris, Mac Traynham, Patsy Edmonds, Bobby Patterson, Benny Jarrell, Becky Haga, Dan Williams, and Willard Gayheart. There was music all afternoon into the evening. A great day!

All this great music and good times—easy to romanticize it all, but living there day to day it became apparent that there was another side, the dark underbelly, as I think of it, that lived uncomfortably with the wonderful music and people. Industrialization in the area had created a situation where many folks went from self-sufficient farming to furniture factory and hosiery mill wages, making people dependent on local industry for a living. Those factories and mills—many of which closed as the jobs were shipped overseas—had created a paternalistic dependency on the whims of bosses, who often were not so concerned with the welfare of their workers. There was a never-ending supply of labor and also considerable effort to keep that labor cheap and keep unions out.

Frank Levering, a writer who had grown up in nearby Orchard Gap, Virginia, left to go to Hollywood and be a screenwriter. There he cowrote the screenplay for the 1982 horror flick *Parasite*—not the 2019 Academy Award-winning one. He eventually returned to take over the family apple orchard and make a film: a love story set against the backdrop of the conflict between the Appalachian Power Company and the local people over a proposed dam, as I remember. Dennis Hopper, Lance Guest, and Mary Elizabeth Mastroianni were to star; musician, songwriter, arranger, and record producer Van Dyke Parks was the music director.

Frank had written the screenplay, had backing, and a plan. He hired Andy and me as musical consultants, he set up auditions (mostly for extras and musicians) in the downtown Galax motel. People were very excited and full of hopes that lives might change, improve, they'd get famous—all of it. This was a big deal! Inevitably there was a lot of gossip, petty rivalries, and rumors along with the fun and excitement. One of the more believable rumors was that the local power structure had made the producers or movie folks agree to not pay any of the local people hired as extras any more than they would make in their factory jobs, so as not to compete with local industry.

I called Wanda Urbanska, who was married to Frank Levering at the time, and she says that this would not have been the case. "Frank was not that kind of person," she told me, "and would never have agreed to such a thing." But the rumor, based in truth, partial truth, or neither, was an indication of how a lot of people felt about the local power structure. In the end, the movie never happened: the backers pulled out and the whole project was axed. Thus ended many Hollywood dreams.

Several of my musical friends from the area, including James Lindsey, Dan and Faye Williams, and Tom Barr, were very pro-union and as active as they could be against what was essentially a brick wall. Dan had a baseball cap that read, "My boss pays me weakly." The local power structure controlled most everything and although there were sporadic attempts to unionize, they all failed. There was definitely a stratified community with doctors, factory owners, and the like at the top and pretty much everybody else at the bottom. I'll never forget something James Lindsey said one time: "Yeah, the Vaughans bring you into the world [at the Vaughan hospital], work you to death [at the Vaughan Furniture factory], and then bury you [at Vaughan Funeral Parlor]."

There was also an attempt at one point to organize musicians against what was seen as a pay-to-play situation when the Moose Lodge, sponsors of the Old Galax Fiddlers Convention, revoked the time-honored tradition of free entry for musicians who competed (essentially getting their entry money back). Suddenly the Moose decided they were not going to give the entry money (or part of it) back to those musicians. A group of us made a flyer that we distributed in the music community.

This effort grew into an organization called the Blue Ridge Music Association, which would sponsor music shows once a month at the Wildlife Club Building a few miles outside of Galax. All the shows were

MUSICIANS !!!

Ask Yourself These Questions :

1 WHY IS THE GALAX MOOSE LODGE DEMANDING FIVE DOLLARS FROM EACH OF YOU AND ALSO YOUR SPOUSES SO THAT YOU CAN PUT ON THEIR SHOW FOR THEM?

2 WHY DOES THE GALAX MOOSE LODGE HOLD A VIRTUAL MONOPOLY ON FIDDL CONVENTIONS IN FELTS PARK?

3 WHY ARE NO ROYALTIES PAID TO MUSICIANS FOR RECORDINGS WHICH THE MOOSE LODGE SELLS?

4 WHY ARE FOLKSINGERS BEING ASKED TO PAY FULL ADMISSION PRICE FC THE PRIVILAGE OF COMPETING?

5 IF THE MOOSE LODGE IS REALLY DEDICATED TO PRESERVING TRADITIC MUSIC OF THIS AREA, WHY DO THEY SEEM TO DISCOURAGE MUSICIANS FROM ATTENDING THE FIDDLERS CONVENTION?

6 ASK YOURSELF THESE QUESTIONS AND DECIDE FOR YOURSELF IF YOU WANT TO SUPPORT AN ORGANIZATION THAT TREATS MUSICIANS IN THIS MAN NER. HOW MUCH ARE MUSICAINS EXPECTED TO CONTRIBUTE BESIDES THEIR TALENT TO PUT ON THIS SHOW FOR THE MOOSE LODGE?

MUSICIANS MAKE THE GALAX FIDDLERS CONVENTION - NOT THE OTHER WAY AROUND

Originial Blue Grass Music

This flyer was put out by the Blue Ridge Music Association in support of musicians' right to get their entry money back if they played in the contest.

free to the public and would feature a couple of bands or musicians—donations were accepted. We would get local stores to donate nabs, country ham, drinks, etc., and one of us would cook the ham and bake the biscuits and we'd serve them from the kitchen at the back of the hall. There was always a big crowd at the shows, and a lot of flatfoot dancing when the music warranted it. We started a Blue Ridge Music Association newsletter that we sent out advertising the shows, musicians, and other music-related stuff of interest to folks in the area.

After I started the *Old-Time Herald*, it became apparent that I'd need more support with technology than was available to me in Galax. I was also getting of a mind to pay more attention to my own music, wherever that took me. So, in 1989 I decided to move to the Triangle area down in North Carolina. I felt a great sense of sadness and loss leaving the area, but I kept my house in Galax so I could come back often, and I did. But eventually my landlord heard on the local radio "Swap and Shop" segment that there was a young couple in need of a place to live and could trade work for rent. He asked me, and I agreed to give up my little home, which seemed like the right thing to do.

For roughly nine years, I had been mentored and befriended by some amazing musicians. So many friendships, so much music. The folks we visited and got to know, who shared with us their lives and music and experiences, many were old, and there were the inevitable goodbyes as they passed on during the time I was there. I will never forget them—folks who shared their music and life stories with us. All of them live in my song "Calling Me Home":

An old friend lay on his dying bed
Held my hand to his dying breast
And he whispered low as I bent my head
"Oh, they're calling me home, they're calling me home."
My time has come to sail away
I know you'd love for me to stay
But I miss my friends of yesterday
"Oh, they're calling me home, they're calling me home."
I know you'll remember me when I'm gone
Remember my stories, remember my songs
I'll leave them on earth, sweet traces of gold
"Oh, they're calling me home, they're calling me home."
So friends gather round and bid me goodbye
My body's bound but my soul shall fly
My little light shinin' from the sky
"Oh, they're calling me home, they're calling me home."

— In and Around Galax —

Bertie Mae Caudill Dickens (1902–94), in her eighties when I knew her, lived in Ennice, North Carolina, a crossroads not far from Galax. From a long line of fiddlers and banjo players, she lived with her lovely and supportive husband Marvin in their small, white frame house along a narrow, rural hardtop road in Alleghany County. In the kitchen of their home was a beautiful wood cookstove that they still used. In a shed in the yard near the kitchen, on shelves lining the walls, were stored jars and jars of canned fruit and vegetables—shining and colorful. Everything was neat and in its place in their home.

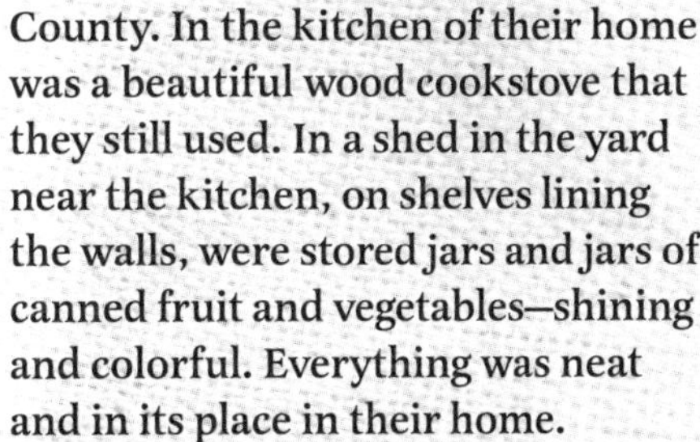

Bert, as we called her, was always "put together," deceptively frail looking—silver hair neatly contained in a hairnet, a pinafore-type apron always worn on top of her dress. She played a monster resonator banjo, and when we came to visit and play music, Marvin or one of us had to drag it out from under the bed and place it in her lap. Her lovely, calm, and stately demeanor was reflected in her banjo playing—"Cleveland Marching to the White House," "Poor Little Johnny's Gone to War," and others. She had a good friend, Faye Wagoner, who would often visit Bert and play guitar with her, and it was extra special if Faye was there when I came by and we had a little trio with fiddle, banjo, and guitar.

In Galax, everyone was a story teller. Bert and Marvin knew Charlie Jarrell, who was Tommy Jarrell's uncle and a fiddler. They knew Charlie because he would come up the mountain from Mount Airy to do business, "trade" and the like, and often stayed the night with them. One night when they were

Ennice, North Carolina, 1985. Bertie Mae Dickens in her usual outfit with apron and hairnet, playing banjo in her living room.

sound asleep, they heard someone stumbling around in their house. It was Charlie, drunk—"Can't find my durn bed!" From the many stories I'd heard about Charlie Jarrell, he was quite a character—a fiddler who loved his moonshine, and who was prone to fits of anger when provoked. One time he couldn't get his fiddle tuned to his liking so he threw it up into a tree; another time one of his toes was bothering him with some kind of bunion till he couldn't stand it, so he put the toe up on a chopping block, chopped it off, and threw it to the dog!

The sweetest woman you'd ever want to meet, Bert loved to play the old tunes that she grew up with, and like most every musician I knew, never or rarely sat down to play by herself. What she enjoyed was playing with others who knew her repertoire or could follow easily. Often when I would drive up, she and Marvin would be sitting in their rockers on the front porch, waiting. In 1992, she received the North Carolina Heritage Award from the North Carolina Arts Council. When Bert died two years later at the age of ninety-two, she and Marvin had been married for seventy-two years.

Matokie Worrell Slaughter (1919–99) was a retired furniture factory worker, a marvelous banjo and fiddle player from a large and lively family of musicians. Matokie had become somewhat known outside the area through the County Records 1960s compilation recordings *Clawhammer Banjo*, volumes 2 and 3.

According to Matokie (her name was Matoka but everyone pronounced it "Matokie"), her mother told her she was named after a Native American woman. I did some cursory research and found that the famous Pocahontas, a member of the Pamunkey tribe, was named Amonute or, more privately, Matoaka. Well, there you go!

I spent a lot of time with Matokie and her husband Ennis (also a retired furniture factory worker) learning her tunes and playing fiddle to her banjo. She and Ennis lived in a small house outside of Pulaski, Virginia, just north of Galax. There were goats, chickens, and dogs, but what I remember most were the guinea hens. As dusk approached, they would fly up into the trees to roost, big shadowy bird lumps lurking there till dawn, when they'd come down and resume foraging and "protecting." In 1987, Andy and I had the chance to take Matokie with us to play at the Kent State Folk Festival in Ohio. We piled into Andy's truck and headed out. Ennis, a diabetic, was riding in the back of the truck and while we stopped at a convenience store, he needed to give himself a shot of insulin, which he proceeded to do in (apparently) full view. Someone saw him and thought he was shooting up drugs and came into the store announcing the fact. I don't remember if we explained what was going on or just hightailed it out of there, but in any event, nobody came after us.

At the festival, groups of young, avid banjo players followed Matokie around, and fiddlers vied for a few minutes to play with her in jam sessions. Later in 1991, Matokie, and I went to play at the Celebration of Traditional Music at Berea College in Kentucky, and in 1992 she and her sister Virgie and I flew to the University of Chicago Folk Festival (the first time either of them had flown).

The Worrell (Matokie's maiden name) family reunions with her noisy, energetic, musical siblings were a treat—brother Mutt and Matokie both played banjo, brother Lum the mandolin. Joe, the youngest, played fiddle, sisters Virgie and Gay played guitar and banjo, and then there were the various friends and neighbors, many of whom played music, all vying for a seat at the musical table. But Matokie, quiet and soft spoken, was definitely the alpha female. There was always lots of food and they sure knew how to have a good time.

Brother Joe had lost all the fingers on his left (noting) hand except the thumb and first in a work accident, and that first finger danced by itself all over the fiddle fingerboard; a listener would never have missed the other fingers! And Joe wore a trucker hat with the inscription "Sworn to fun, loyal to none!"

In 1990, Matokie, Virgie (Richardson) Worrell, and I (the "Back Creek Buddies," we called ourselves) made a cassette tape, *Saro*.

Pulaski, Virginia, 1990. Virgie Richardson (*center*), Matokie's sister; Matokie (*right*); and I were having pictures taken for the cover of a cassette tape we were making of the music we played together. Photo by Wayne Martin.

Andy Cahan wrote the following notes when I later reissued it on CD: "[Matokie] was much like her music—rock solid, but with a gentle nature. Her family was an extended clan of lively musicians, always welcoming and warm, full of enthusiasm, and devoid of pretense. In their midst, Matokie seemed unaware of her singularity as a musician. Long after she has left us, [her] music still stands as an inspiration to further generations of old-time musicians."

An interesting side note to Matokie's story is that during the 1990s Margaret Kilgallen, a young San Francisco artist and lover of traditional music, had heard Matokie, probably on one of the County records, and was completely taken with her music. Kilgallen began drawing graffiti on freight trains ("tagging") using the name "Matokie" as an homage to the original Matokie Slaughter. Sadly, Kilgallen died of cancer in 2001. In the Aspen Art Museum hardcover catalog, *Margaret Kilgallen: that's where the beauty is*, accompanying an exhibit of Kilgallen's work in 2019, Jenelle Porter wrote, "[Kilgallen] remarked on how few women tagged trains. She knew she was one of only a handful and that adding to the conversation indicated her full-hearted adoration for the anachronistic and the under-sung. The names she used on those trains were Matokie Slaughter, M. Slaughter, M.S., and Matokie. Matokie . . . was the first woman Kilgallen ever heard playing old-time music. . . . She broadcast Slaughter's name on train cars and in installations. Looking at the work now, the word 'Slaughter' in ten-foot capital letters is more than a memorialization; it's a proclamation."

Around 1987, I started playing fiddle with ***Enoch Rutherford*** (1916–2004), who lived in the Gold Hill section on a small farm near Independence, Virginia, not far from Galax. Enoch played fiddle too, but mostly he was known as a banjo player around those parts. A man of competitive nature who loved to win at fiddlers conventions, he often won with the tune "Sugar Hill": "I've won more ribbons on that than any a tune I've played, yessir." Enoch, a widower, lived by himself, was a chain smoker and a man filled with lore, stories, and unexpected pieces of knowledge. He always liked to have at least one woman in his band, and when he asked me at some point to join the Gold Hill Band as fiddler, I was thrilled.

That incarnation of the Gold Hill Band was Enoch, me, Carol Holcomb on guitar, and Dale Morris on bass. I learned a lot of great tunes from Enoch, but mostly how to play fast (I can't play that fast anymore). He tore that banjo up, and when he took out on "Sally Ann" or "Greasy Meat," you had to get on it! We played dances, little local festivals and gatherings, on the radio from time to time, and made one tape, *Old Cap'n Rabbit*. Enoch loved to play—anywhere, any time.

I had an interest in finding out about any African American banjo or fiddle players who might have been around during the time Enoch and others were learning to play, and when I visited older musicians, I invariably asked them if they remembered any African Americans from the old days who played string music. Enoch mentioned several, all banjo players: Crockett Phipps, Greek MacMillan, and Leonard McKinney were some he mentioned—all long gone. Kelly Lundy, son of legendary Galax fiddler Emmett Lundy, and a fine guitar player and singer, mentioned a Black fiddler, Calvin Maxwell, a contemporary of Emmett Lundy. Kelly's gone now and I wish I'd asked him more. There may be more on the tapes at the Southern Folklife Collection, and maybe someone could do some research.

Enoch talked about when he worked in the steel mills in Pennsylvania during World War II, and, like so many other Southerners living and working there, would often go to Sunset Park in Chester County to hear the kind of music that took him home. One time he and I rode around the countryside near where he lived in the Gold Hill community, and he talked about nature, animals, plants, medicine, and the way life used to be.

I was visiting Enoch once and noticed a strange, little table in his front room. It was fairly rudimentary—a twelve-by-twenty-four-inch plywood top, four legs, but at the bottom of each leg was attached a turkey claw! I was all over that thing, and he said he'd make me one. A few weeks later I came back to visit and pick up my table and Enoch informed me that he'd gone out and shot the wild turkeys (so he could use the feet), hung them up on his porch to dry, and his dog got them and ate them. Enoch had to kill a chicken (actually two) and made the table with chicken instead of turkey feet. I loved that little clawfoot table.

Banjo player Enoch Rutherford from up around the Gold Hill area near Independence, Virginia, 1987. Along with Dale Morris and Carol Holcomb, we played together as The Gold Hill Band.

Kahle Brewer (1904–89) was a fiddler who recorded back in the mid-1920s for Victor and OKeh Records with Ernest V. Stoneman and others. He lived with his wife, Edna, just outside of Galax, a mile or so as the crow flies from my house. Craig Johnson, a fine fiddle and banjo player and songwriter (Double Decker Stringband), and a longtime friend from my DC days, would often make the trip to Galax to spend some time with the elders, and we'd always stop by and visit Kahle—pronounced "Kale"—and Edna. Sometimes Kahle was a little reluctant about playing since he had a tremor in his right arm and couldn't always control the bow like he wanted. Being a proud man, it often took persuading—we didn't *care* that his fiddling wasn't as technically perfect as it had been. When he did play for us, we could hear that old lilting sound—the sound that took us back to those old recordings, a style rarely heard any more.

Otis Burris (1917–89) was a champion fiddler and flatfoot dancer, known for his beautiful rendition of the tune "Fortune"— "Once I had a fortune, kept it in a trunk. Lost it all a-gambling one night when I got drunk."

Otis had lived a hard, alcohol-fueled life in his younger days but had quit drinking and lived quietly with his wife Cora in downtown

Kahle Brewer, Galax, Virginia, 1987.

Otis Burris (*left*) with Eldridge Montgomery (*right*) on Otis's front porch in downtown Galax, 1988.

Galax. With the help and encouragement of his old friend and bandmate from the local prize-winning Mountain Ramblers, James Lindsey ("rich folks spell it with an 'a'; mine's spelled with an 'e'"), he started to play again. He and James formed a bluegrass band—Otis Burris & Fortune, with Otis on fiddle as the focal point, James on rhythm mandolin, Eldridge Montgomery and me on guitars and vocals, Wendell Cockerham on banjo, and Hilary Dirlam on bass. We played on the radio, at gatherings and local shows all around the area and we made a tape, *Otis Burris and Fortune*. I loved singing with Eldridge. He had one of those old-time bluegrass voices—a bit of Lester Flatt, a bit of Carter Stanley. Eldridge and I sang at Otis's funeral in 1989.

I would occasionally get together with Helen Cockram (d. 2021) and Carol Rogers. Both Helen and Carol were good singers, and our idea was to work out three-part harmony on a bunch of songs and maybe do a show at the Wildlife Club at some point. I have tapes of our rehearsals that bring back a lot of memories—lots of laughter and some good singing, too. Helen was a good songwriter and had written several gospel songs and ballads.

Nell Smith (d. 2018) was a singer who worked in the spray room of the local furniture factory, never married, and took care of her mother till her death. Nell was tough (you had to be to work in the spray room), lived on her own, and ran a small trailer park behind her house. I remember she had a head of thick, dark hair and loved to sing and write songs. She wasn't a ballad singer or a singer of old songs; she sang songs that she wrote. She had a cutting, strong voice and knew what she liked. Nell wrote some memorable songs including one that Kay Justice, Gail Gillespie, and I recorded on our album *Tear Down the Fences*, "The Devil's Gonna Meet You Down at the Old Still," in which a woman socks it to a no-good drunken husband by pouring his jar of white liquor into the outhouse toilet, and other adventures. "All those years you said you'd drink no more, I'd like to bust you with a two by four," was one line of a song full of quotable lyrics.

There are many folks most people have never heard of, hidden away in small communities, who are songwriters as well as players. They often write about their homes, their communities, and their life experiences within those communities, and so on. Nell was one of these. So was Othar Fortner from Fries (a bit the other side of Galax—"It's Freeze or Fries depending on the time of year," people would say). Fortner wrote about local subjects—beans, cornbread, and the early recording artist and Fries native Henry Whitter of Grayson & Whitter. Fortner put out a cassette tape of his songs, which was a local hit.

Another memorable songwriter was Gene Carpenter, who was originally from Kentucky but had moved to the Galax area and had written (and recorded) "They'll Never Land a Man on the Sun." I have a 45 rpm recording of it that I cherish. It's also available online.

Nell Smith singing one of her songs at the Wildlife Club show, a monthly event just outside Galax run by local musicians, ca. 1986.

Laurel Fork, Virginia, 1987. The home of banjo player Martin Marshall and his wife, Eula. Built by Martin's father, it was the local post office for a while.

Martin Marshall (1905–96) lived with his wife Eula in his old homeplace (built by his father with logs and siding and which, for a while, also served as the local post office) near Laurel Fork, Virginia. I first heard of Martin through a wonderful LP, *The Bell Spur String Band*, and through local enthusiast Elbert Marshall, who had recorded them and put the recordings out on Bobby Patterson's local Heritage label. Martin played in an index finger lead style as opposed to the more often played clawhammer style, and basically followed a fiddle lead. He and Eula also had a collection of songs that they loved to sing, and she had this weird doll collection arrayed on her upstairs bed, reminiscent of something from a Stephen King story. Gail Gillespie remembers that Eula had once remarked that she would like to be buried with her dolls. Gail and I would often go to visit Eula and Martin after I moved to Durham. After Martin died, we went up to visit Eula. We brought our instruments and played some of the tunes we'd learned from Martin on fiddle and banjo. While we were playing, Eula dialed up a friend to let her hear us, saying how much she was enjoying our playing Martin's music, and how many good memories it brought back.

Singer ***Hurley Hampton*** was ninety-three and lived in the Baywood section outside of Galax when I visited him in 1986. I think Luther Davis may have put me onto Hurley. He used to play the banjo but had stopped. We talked a lot . . . about other players from the area that he liked, about sitting up with bodies at a wake, keeping the bodies cool, and about singing at wakes. We talked about his job at the livestock market, where he worked for forty-seven years weighing cattle, about dances they used to have in his house, and about his wife who had died recently . . . then he launched into singing with his old, beautiful voice. He sang a lot of religious songs like "When I Can Read My Titles Clear" and "The Nazarene" (he was a Primitive Baptist), but he knew others like "Claude Allen," "The Blind Child," and "Sinful to Flirt," among them.

Dan Tate (1896–1990) lived in Fancy Gap, in Carroll County, Virginia. Andy and I went to visit him in 1984. His home was very dark, blinds drawn, with little light. It didn't bother him a bit; he was legally blind and wore thick glasses, but I remember the darkness and the difficulty of taking photos with so little light. Dan was a brilliant banjo player and singer who learned many of his songs and tunes from his mother and older sister. He referred to one of the banjo tunings he used as "deep mountain." Like so many of the old-timers, he credited the people from whom he learned his songs: "one of my old Uncle Joshua Tate's songs. . . . I knew ['Walk Jawbone'] as a banjo/fiddle tune, but a visitor wrote the words down for me, said it came from Alabama."

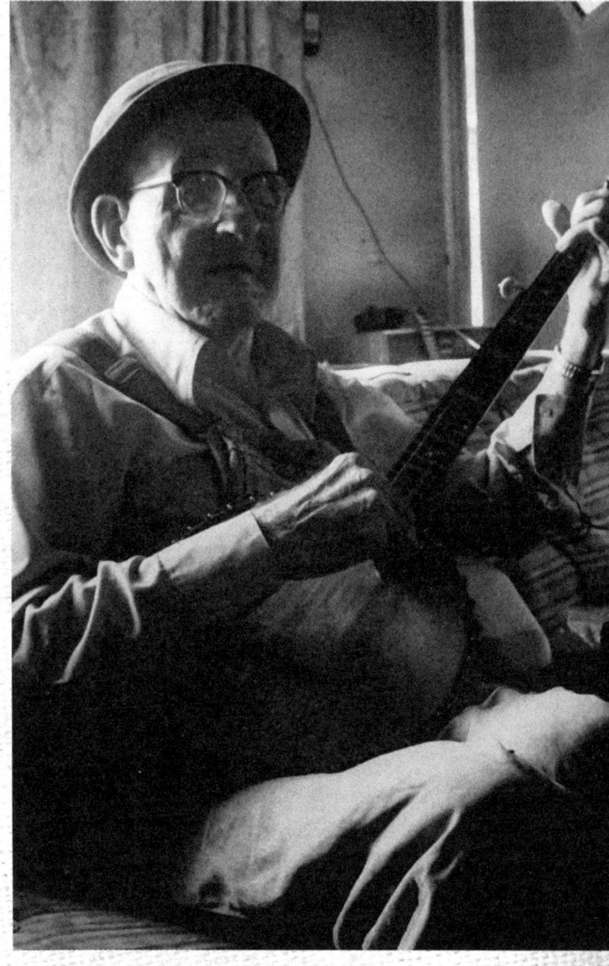

Dan Tate at home in Fancy Gap, Virginia, 1984.

I think of ***Wayne Lowe***, the shy, sweet fiddler from around Fancy Gap, Parley Parsons and John Patterson in Carroll County, Art Wooten over in Sparta, NC (Bill Monroe's first fiddler in 1939), and so many more. There were the folks up around Whitetop above Independence, Virginia—fiddle maker and player Albert Hash and his daughter Audrey who learned to make fiddles alongside her dad; Emily and Thornton Spencer, husband and wife team, banjo and fiddle players who were responsible for spreading around a lot of the music from their area in Grayson and Smyth Counties, forming classes in the schools up on Whitetop and holding evening classes that older folks could attend to learn or just get together and play. Albert, Emily, and Thornton, along with Tom and Becky Barr from Galax, formed the Whitetop Mountain Band, a popular string band that played a lot locally, recorded, and became known well beyond Southwest Virginia. Although Thornton passed in 2017, Emily remains very active today, along with their musical children Kilby and Martha Spencer.

Thornton Spencer, fiddler with the Whitetop Mountain Band, based in the mountains around Whitetop, Virginia. I took this photo at a bluegrass festival in Hoboken, Georgia, in 1983.

Emily Spencer's banjo class, Whitetop, Virginia, ca. 1987. Emily is seated lower right.

FAMILY MATTERS

Someone reading this might ask, "What about your kids?" I was doing what I wanted, but how were they faring? We kept in touch, and I went to DC occasionally and they came down occasionally, but it wasn't the same as being close by. I think of families who stay in their communities, being to some extent dependent on one another to help with work, children, and the like. I certainly wasn't that person and had not grown up in that kind of family. Later, when grandchildren came, although I didn't live nearby I "stepped up to the plate and was involved," as my daughter Jenny said. We visited back and forth; I often took care of them and we would do fun things together.

It's funny how "doing your own thing," especially for women, can often bring guilt and some regret about how your choices affect your children's lives. I'm proud of all my children. They had a hard row to hoe as they say, but came through—a plumber, a couple of teachers, and a doctor—maybe a little scarred, but successful, generally happy with their lives, and with children of their own—my grandchildren whom I love dearly.

It was always rewarding to find women musicians near where I lived in the Galax area, it being a very traditional community in many ways—where women did the domestic labor of cooking, child-rearing, cleaning, and washing. But I met women like Bertie Mae Dickens and Matokie Slaughter who were married and had kids and always made music, and I met women like Leone Parish and Nell Smith who never married, worked, and always made music. It was common among many of the men I met for them to have given up music when they had a family and worked a job; they would come back to it later, as did Tommy Jarrell. Women were known as singers, and carried on ballad traditions, but I also heard countless mentions of women fiddlers and banjo players. They might have been someone's mother who taught them banjo or fiddle, or it might be a woman who was known as a player but played mostly at home and not out at dances or public functions. I'm not talking about professional women players and singers like Lily May Ledford, the Carter Family, Cousin Emmy, Molly O'Day, and the like. I'm talking about the countless women hidden away in small communities, working at home, on the farm, or sometimes the factory, women whom we may never hear about except that someone you talk to speaks of them and remembers them.

My time in Galax was between 1981 and 1989. Since then, things have changed a lot with the loss of the hosiery mills when they went overseas. The area has seen the closing of many businesses, the opening of others, and the town trying to make itself viable with all of the shifting in the economy. One of the strengths of the area has been, I firmly believe, its music and its people. I had a long talk with Marianne Kovatch, associate director of the Blue Ridge Music center near Galax. She is also an old-time banjo player. We talked about all this and the various changes that have taken place since I left. I asked her if she would weigh in here:

> Many of the communities in the area suffered when the textile and furniture industries closed their doors, but they have been slowly coming back . . . there is still some furniture and textile manufacturing, but it is no longer the main economic driver. . . . The local music has changed over the years. The old [generation] is gone, and family music links are broken for the most part, with kids learning to play in after-school Junior Appalachian Musician classes [a program founded by Helen White around 2009] rather than having it passed down from family and neighbors. . . . The love of dancing remains the same—you still see people of all ages get up to flatfoot and two step to the music, with the young people learning by watching and imitating what they see.
>
> Fiddlers' Conventions are still held . . . throughout the summer, but several long-standing conventions are slowly dying out as fewer people are attending. . . . The Galax Old Fiddlers Convention, sponsored by the local Moose Lodge, is still the largest and oldest, but others have or are in danger of folding. Community jams have blossomed and help to bring the musicians together and keep the local traditions going . . . There are lots of varying opinions about the changes and I'm sure there are endless discussions as to whether the changes are good, beneficial to the people, the music, the traditions. . . . Still, they were inevitable, and necessary to keep the area alive. I'd love to hear what James Lindsey would have to say about it all.

Thanks, Marianne. I'd love that, too.

Saturday, April 8, 1967 THE DAILY TAR HEEL Page 5

'China' Poplin leans against a pick-up truck and picks a happy banjo style for the delighted crowd. Bearded Frank George, left, fiddles with the sad far-away look that mystifies all who hear and see him.

Old Time Fiddlers' Convention

By JOCK LAUTERER AND BECKY SCOTT

As joyously as the first day of spring, the Union Grove Fiddlers' Convention [illegible] into being each Easter week-end with the happy crackle and spit of the Bluegrass fiddle and banjo.

From out of the green hills and smoky cities of the east coast came the fiddlers and strummers to converge on the tiny Iredale community of Union Grove.

And from the same hills and cities come the listeners. As varied as their transportation, they came in Sting Rays, '38 coupes and Harley Davidson Duro-Glides.

The near 10,000 pitched tents and set up camp in cow pastures, playgrounds and empty fields, swelling the cross roads to a musical boom town.

A relaxed Saturday afternoon crowd of listeners strolled around between knots of performers, choosing their favorites from among Nashville stompers, Mountain fiddlers and Bluegrass banjo players.

Eona and China Poplin of Sumpter, S. C. leaned against a battered pick-up truck and offered gleeful renditions of "Don't put no sales tax on the women," and "You ain't woman enough to taky my man."

Tall and dark in his black bowler, solemn Roger Sprung presented "progressive Bluegrass": a sophisticated version of the Real Thing modified by commercialism and knowledge of music theory.

[illegible] younger [illegible] played the traditional Bluegrass with cool condescension towards their more enthusiastic elders.

The view from the hot-dog stand was of an immense musical zoo, pulsing and screeching with unrestrained enthusiasm.

The college students with guitars beat a hasty retreat to their tents to pick out PP&M songs, which seemed strangely pale and out of place in this setting.

The actual competition began in the evening, with each of the 83 groups playing in the gym, the auditorium and the tent. The gym and the auditorium had lighting and acoustics but the tent had atmosphere. Bread-bagging swingers and sober old-timers joined in appreciative foot-stomping.

This was North Carolina at its happiest. It was a gathering of talented folk and interested observers who enjoyed themselves and each other.

Those who insist that the folk arts in North Carolina are dead have only to look to the Union Grove Fiddlers' Convention to see that these arts are not just [illegible] flourishing.

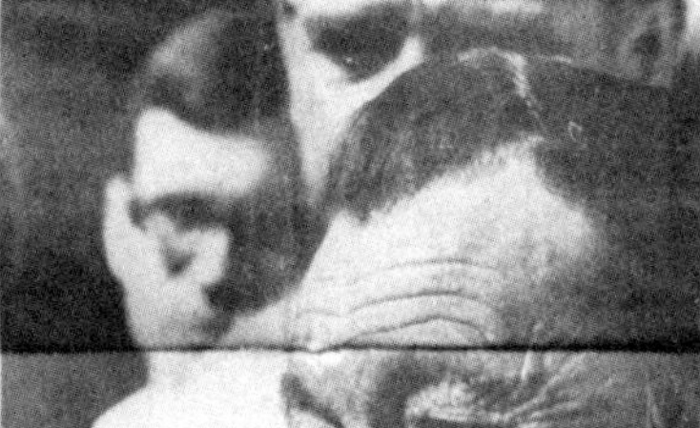

'Otis' of the Galax Mountain Ramblers—his face and fiddlin' command attention.

Out of the hills come the blues and Bluegrass strummers, providing ample fascination for Union Grove children.

Photos by Jock Lauterer

George Pegram sings with more soul than most folks have to start out with: "Joooohnnnnn Ennnnn-ryyyyy-was aaaaaaaaa-little-uh-baaaabe . . . Goooon- nna-die with maa haaamaah in ma hand looooordy-looordy . . . Pollyyyy Anne drove steel lak a maaaan."

DOWN IN NORTH CAROLINA

After I moved down to Durham and the *Old-Time Herald* got kind of sorted out, I met and started visiting and playing with some wonderful traditional musicians; folks like Joe and Odell Thompson from Mebane, Etta Baker and her sister Cora Phillips from Caldwell County, Lauchlin Shaw from Harnett County, and his music buddy A. C. Overton, who lived near Raleigh. And I would continue to visit old friends up the mountain as much as possible. I played music a lot with the many younger musicians around the Triangle area, forming several iterations of bands that included good musicians like John Worthington, Al McCanless, Robert Truesdale, Donnie Evans, Mark Weems, Nancy Gottovi, and others. We concentrated on country, country blues, and original material for the most part. Sharon Sandomirsky, Gail Gillespie, and I formed an old-time band called the Herald Angels

FACING An article in the April 8, 1967, issue of UNC's *Daily Tar Heel* about the Galax Fiddlers Convention. Otis Burris is pictured in the center, right.

ABOVE Joe Thompson playing fiddle with his cousin Odell on banjo, ca. 1988.

Cora Phillips (*left*) and Etta Baker, 1990.

because the three of us were associated in some way with the magazine. There were local venues—Pyewacket, Columbia Street Bakery, there was a place in Hillsborough whose name I've forgotten, and so many other places, many gone now. The Red Clay Ramblers and the Green Level Entertainers, and many others were very active in the area and beyond, and there was lots going on musically. The *Old-Time Herald* got a grant to help MerleFest feature more traditional music, and as a result we ran the Traditional and Dance tents for many years.

Chapter 7

THE OLD-TIME HERALD; OR, HOW (NOT?) TO START A MAGAZINE

Often, friends and I would sit around playing music in my small Galax kitchen, drinking and talking in between tunes. The conversations would run to the future of old-time music. What if there were a niche magazine for old-time music much like *Bluegrass Unlimited* (*BU*) for bluegrass? Seemed like a good idea. I founded the *Old-Time Herald* in 1987 after many sleepless nights wondering what I was going to do next in this life. It was 1986 or thereabouts and I was living in Galax, working with Andy Cahan on a recording project documenting three musician friends. During visits from friends, playing music and talking in my kitchen, the conversations would often run to the future of old-time music. Where was it headed? Who was the old-time music community? Did people playing the music understand where it came from, appreciate the generations of musicians before them? A thought took hold and gnawed at and worried my mind. What if *I* started a magazine? I've never been one to think I *couldn't* do something if I really wanted to. So I decided to jump off the cliff and do it. When an idea takes hold in the middle of the night and you can't sleep, and the next night, and the next—you'd better act. With about $2,000 of my own money and another $4,000 from friends, no knowledge of publishing, computers, printing, or basically anything related to putting out a magazine, I went stubbornly forward.

I had been involved in the birth of *Bluegrass Unlimited*, the premier magazine dedicated to bluegrass music, which came about in much the same way—because of meetings of musicians and fans who were concerned about the future of bluegrass and wanted to further its reach. In 1966, with Pete Kuykendall, a musician, record collector, entrepreneur, and driving force at the helm, it got underway, starting as a mimeographed eight-by-seventeen several-page rag. It soon became apparent that the magazine was a success, providing a forum for discussions (Should the Osborne Brothers use an electric bass??? That was a hot one!). It provided announcements of events and who was playing where, and reviews of recordings—it focused on the community. Over the years, *BU* became a slick, glossy-color-cover, well-respected magazine, and it continues today.

I didn't know the first thing about putting out a magazine, but I did know a lot of people who might help me. I talked with folks and found an affordable printer. I called historian, folklorist, and writer Charles Wolfe (d. 2006) and persuaded him to be an adviser and to write a piece for the magazine's first issue. I got "testimonials" from various folks, including Ramona Jones, Garrison Keillor, John Hartford, Ola Belle Reed, and others, saying the magazine was a good idea. There was universal support in the old-time music and academic communities for the concept of the magazine.

Bobby Patterson (1942–2017), a friend born and raised in Galax (his father John was an old-time fiddler), was a bluegrass guitarist and banjoist who loved old-time music and was devoted to the musical heritage of the area.

Bobby was also the owner and founder of Heritage Records and a small store, the Heritage Shoppe, in Galax, which boasted a "large selection of Wilton cake and candy-making supplies, partyware, wedding accessories and invitations, stringed instruments, and hard-to-find bluegrass music on cd and cassette." He let me use, rent-free, the basement of the Heritage Shoppe as an office, move in a desk and filing cabinet, and set up business. Conveniently, the Woodlawn post office was just down the road. Mind you, this post office was very small, serviced a small rural community, and Postmaster Clarence Davis had never dealt much with out-of-the-ordinary situations like our bulk mailings, so he periodically (when he saw us coming with postal bags of the magazine) freaked out a bit, but stoically got the magazine mailed out. Over the years we have had a lot of experience with the US Postal Service and learned that as in all bureaucracies, one question might bring ten different answers. It was critical to identify friends within the USPS structure and learn to work with them. If they were on your side everything was pretty good; if not, it could be pretty bad.

From the very first, I had a definite idea of what the magazine should be, and with the editorial in the first issue tried to clarify my goals: "devoted to the support, promotion, and encouragement of old-time music . . . a vehicle for bringing together ideas, to give voice to old-time musicians and fans, to publish articles of interest (historical and contemporary), and to review old-time music recordings and tapes. We will pay attention to record companies, festivals, radio, etc., that support and present old-time music in a way consistent with the respect that it deserves . . . national in scope. . . ."

I also felt that the magazine should have a color cover, glossy pages, not mimeographed as *BU* was when it started out, and felt that this would make it more credible. I felt strongly that it shouldn't be a fan magazine or an academic publication but should present articles of interest and importance, that it should reach out not just to aficionados but to many different people, and that it should be accessible to all. I felt strongly that reviews should be critical. They were intended to reflect the state of the art and not just be fanzine-style reviews. This generated, as readers of the *OTH* over the years will know, some outraged responses and hurt feelings. Old-time music had rarely been subjected to critical examination except perhaps in the *Little Sandy Review* (1959–65), founded

Bobby Patterson, Galax, Virginia, ca. 1990.

and edited by Jon Pankake (d. 2023) and Paul Nelson (d. 2006). They stated in the introduction to their first issue, "We are two people who love folk music very much and want to do all we can to help the good in it grow and the bad in it perish. After reading this issue, it should be very apparent to anyone who we think is good and who we think is bad and why." Jon Pankake agreed to review for the *OTH* and did so for many years.

I wanted there to be a gender balance among the writers, and in what the *OTH* wrote about, and for it to reflect African American and other minority folk traditions as well as Anglo.

I felt that in the *OTH* there should be discussion of issues that were important to old-time musicians and the future of old-time music, hence the Issues in Old-Time Music column wherein took place the long-running, heated discussion generated by Mac Benford's "Folklorists & Us" article and Joe Wilson's response, a debate about the roles of folklorists and "revivalist" musicians that started in 1989 and continued burning up the pages of the Issues column until mid-1990.

Technology was a huge problem for me. I had barely gotten used to an electric typewriter, and it soon became apparent that I'd need to be able to generate a mailing list, keep track of it, and print it when the magazine was ready to mail. Patrick Sky (1940–2021), a noted folk musician and friend, with whom I'd spoken, suggested an Atari computer, which had a decent mailing program.

After I got the computer (by mail), I spent many frustrating hours throwing things at the wall and cursing, trying to figure out how to use the damn thing (I never have been and am still not good with how-to manuals). No one in Galax had computers (or at least, no one I knew), and no one had a clue or could help me. Fortunately, a friend in Chapel Hill was computer savvy and offered to help me achieve some kind of technological enlightenment. I'd load the Atari into the car, drive the three hours down the mountain and into the Piedmont to Amy Jones's house. We'd spend several hours, she'd set me up, I'd watch, listen, take notes, then load it back into the car and drive home. This happened several times before I finally got to where the computer and I could function fairly well together.

When it was finally done, the editorial in the first issue read—

> This is the first issue of a new magazine to be devoted to the support, promotion, and encouragement of old-time music. The intent of the *Old-Time Herald* is to provide a vehicle for bringing together ideas, to give voice to old-time musicians and fans, to publish articles of interest (historic and contemporary), and to

review old-time music recordings and tapes. . . . The *Old-Time Herald* will be national in scope. . . . There is old-time music everywhere, and we will try to let you know what is going on. The main focus . . . will be the traditional old-time fiddle, banjo, and vocal music of the southeastern United States— a musical tradition which has also spread over large portions of the west, midwest, the Ozark region and other areas. . . . This rich musical genre currently includes not only a wealth of traditional musicians both young and old, but several new popular movements. Therefore, in addition to our primary focus on traditional old-time music, we intend to include articles on these popular forms and on eclectic music and other musical traditions which draw on old-time music for inspiration. . . . We will also include occasional articles on traditional bluegrass music as well as various other forms whose development and context in many ways parallel that of southeastern old-time music. . . ."

The *Old-Time Herald* booth celebrating the first issue at the Galax Fiddlers Convention, 1987. Seated behind the table is Evelyn Farmer, a fine singer and autoharp player, and Dale Morris, a friend who was instrumental in helping with the OTH and played bass with us in Enoch Rutherford's Gold Hill Band. He's on the recordings we made with Enoch (on cassette tape).

The editorial ended with a thanks to supporters and contributors and a dedication "to the memory of all the old-time musicians who have passed on—and to those who are carrying it on."

The first issue included an interview with the Slate Mountain Ramblers, a Galax-area string band; musician and writer Hilary Dirlam contributed an article on the Western North Carolina fiddler Bruce Greene; and Phil Jamison said he would like to edit a regular column on dance, that we called the Dance Beat. Linda Higginbotham wrote an article that attempted to define old-time music (which became somewhat controversial). We had a slate of reviews by talented writers, and I was able to fill editorial positions with friends and colleagues who were also experts in the field.

Within six months of the idea being born, the first issue saw the light of day at the August 1987 Galax Fiddlers Convention. I had a trade agreement with the Moose Lodge that ran the convention—a free ad in trade for an *OTH* table at the convention, an agreement kept for many years. Companies like County Sales, Autumn Wind, and Bernunzio Vintage Instruments advertised with us faithfully over the years.

THE BUSINESS OF PUBLISHING

Letters in the first issue reflected people's support as they began to hear about this new magazine.

> While I was in Nashville at John Hartford's . . . he gave me a copy of your letter to him about the *Old-Time Herald*. . . . I'm for anyone or anything that will help spread the word and get the attention of people about old-time music. . . . Good luck with your magazine.—Elmer Bird, Kentucky

> Thanks for trying to establish a forum that has great potential.—Rob Golan, North Carolina

> Great idea! I look forward to your magazine with panting breath and frothing mouth.—Armin Barnett, Washington

> Enclosed find $10 for a one-year subscription to the *OTH*. . . . Do you know the names and addresses of persons who have any back issues to sell of my old *Cowboy Music World* magazine that I formerly published in the 1940s? I was known then as Texas Frank.—Frank Karpinski, New York

Quite a bit later during some discussion or other—probably an *OTH* board meeting where the talk always turned to money, how to get it, and why didn't we ever have it—the subject of how the magazine got started came up. I said that it might have been better if I'd gone in with a partner type who knew about business. Someone replied that yes, that might have been a good idea, but that business knowledge might have kept me from starting the magazine—and I never would have done it had I known.

As it was, with dedicated volunteers, talented writers and record reviewers, and folks who love the music all pitching in, we launched the very first issue in August 1987. And over the years, the fun of writing and soliciting articles and editing the *Old-Time Herald* turned out to be only part of the job. Dealing with mailing permits and the USPS and its zones, zip codes, third-class mail, laying out the magazine (at the time it was cutting up wax strips of printed copy and laying them onto sheets of 8 × 11-inch paper), bagging magazines, and fundraising were not fun, but necessary. Every couple of months I'd put together, edit, and type up the magazine copy, collect the ads and photos, and drive it all up to Salem, Virginia, to Dooley Printers. They would typeset everything, I would go up and collect it all and proofread it, then take it back up—a round trip of around 170 miles (gas was cheaper then). They would lay it out, I would go up and check it all, and when the magazine was printed, I'd go back up and pick up boxes of magazines to bring back to the Heritage Shoppe to label, bag up and take to the postmaster at Woodlawn who, again, was *not* happy to see me come.

My experience in the business and organizational side of things was nil. The money came in, the money went out, and I paid myself a small salary out of what came in, but basically it was and always has been, a labor of love. At some point along the way I conferred with friends and decided we should become a nonprofit, since the mailing costs (one of the major expenses) would be much less. I won't bore you with the details of how this was accomplished; suffice it to say that we became a 501c3 nonprofit entity named the Old-Time Music Group in early 1989.

It also became apparent around the same time, as someone pointed out to me, that as a nonprofit we were going to have to form a board of directors and have meetings, do fundraising and be a real organization with bylaws. In March 1989, I decided to move to Durham, North Carolina, feeling that there would be more resources for the magazine and the organization in a more metropolitan area. In April, right after I moved, there was a "Sounds of the South" conference at UNC in Chapel Hill to celebrate the opening of the Southern Folklife Collection at UNC-Chapel Hill with the John Edwards Memorial Collection.

The conference lasted for several days. Lots of luminaries of the folk academic, musical, and writing and publishing communities attended. I felt that I needed help defining how the magazine would proceed, its goals, how it should be run, where it should be heading, and that many of these folks would have a lot to say that could be helpful. Several friends of the *OTH* and I organized a meeting to which we invited many of the folks attending the conference: Margaret Martin volunteered her brother's house for the meeting, and Archie Green, Pete Kuykendall, Tony Russell, George Holt, and Sharon Sandomirsky were among those who attended. We had snacks and coffee and sat around in the living room and discussed the *OTH*. I taped the meeting, which lasted all afternoon as I remember, and later someone transcribed it for me. That transcription is around somewhere, probably in the Southern Folklife Collection. Many of the details are hazy in my mind, but I remember two remarks in particular: Archie Green being aghast that we had incorporated in Delaware—"It looks bad; the perception is that there's something underhanded about it," and Pete Kuykendall saying, "You've GOT to separate your money from the organization money." As a result of that meeting, I started to try and get my ducks in a row; a bona fide board of directors and advisory board was formed.

At that time the advisory board consisted of Ray Alden, Mac Benford, Hazel Dickens, Bobby Fulcher, John Hartford, Linda Higginbotham, Ramona Jones, Garrison Keillor, Brad Leftwich, W. K. McNeil, Pete Sutherland, and Charles Wolfe. The board of directors were Jack Bernhardt, Robert Cantwell, me, Art Menius, Jim Watson, and Kathy World.

Garrison Keillor served for several years on the advisory board, and wrote us a lovely letter to use for fundraising:

> The *Herald* in just three years has become a valuable (and enjoyable) magazine dedicated to traditional American music, and I look forward to it four times a year. . . . In the years when I did "A Prairie Home Companion," so many wonderful folk musicians came across our stage from all over America, good people who appreciated the diversity of the American heritage and who treasured their piece of it and who delighted to show it to others. This same spirit lives on in the *Herald* as well as a keen scholarly curiosity and fine critical sensibility that are rare and therefore vitally important in this field. . . . Alice Gerrard is the founder, editor, and driving force behind the *Herald*, a powerful musician and writer and a dedicated advocate of old-time and bluegrass

> music. She is certainly the right person to be heading up this endeavor. . . . I hope you can help our organization as it looks for financial assistance.

My old friend Ralph Rinzler offered this note of praise for the magazine:

> As a performer, folklorist and founder of the Smithsonian Institution's research and presentation programs in this field, I have worked for 35 years to promote knowledge and appreciation of the authentic folk music of the United States. . . . The Old-Time Music Group has initiated an effective means of nurturing these important artistic traditions both within the community of musicians nationwide and among the general public. . . . I have known Alice Gerrard for more than 30 years. She has been thoroughly devoted to the perpetuation of traditional music for most of her life and has made significant contributions as an artist and advocate. She is a brilliant musician in her own right, and an inspired and effective organizer. I can assure you that her work with the Old-Time Music Group is eminently deserving of support, and that any assistance you may provide will directly benefit the cultural life of our country.

I don't know about "effective organizer" but I'm proud that Ralph thought so.

We wrote up a mission statement and bylaws, and fortunately one of the new board members was able to get us a Macintosh computer. We applied for and received a small grant so I could learn how to lay out the magazine in PageMaker, and we were off and running.

For all of the time that I was the editor and main employee—with whatever irritations and frustrations and hard work—it was an amazing trip. Eventually, we could afford to hire a part-time assistant, some for several years and some for a few months. There were many wonderful and strange stories, many rewards, and many experiences I would have never had without the *OTH*. We got lots of letters complaining about not receiving the magazine (delivery glitches) and many gratifying letters in response to articles. Some of the most gratifying were the ones from a son or granddaughter of some old-timer we'd written about, letting us know how touched they were by the article, and wanting us to know they were proud of their heritage and how they appreciated having it acknowledged in the pages of the magazine. I recently went back through a file labeled "weird stuff" containing mostly letters of an odd nature the *OTH* received over the years. There were letters from paranoid readers informing on people they thought were ripping musicians off: "We must clean up country music by warning each other about the worst of these thieves, liars, crooks, and dream smashers. . . . They prey on unsuspecting singers and songwriters. . . . They are bottom feeders like the scum sucking carp, which they resemble," or from readers complaining that they were left out or ignored by a musical "elite." One such letter was titled "Jamming at Mt. Airy [fiddlers convention]": "Ironic to watch the very icons who work to perpetuate the future of old-time music, ordaining its slow death by presiding over cliquey and exclusive jam sessions . . . tight little circles of special people."

There was one series of letters in particular—one of the wonderful sequences of events that I would never have experienced were it not for the *OTH*. We got a letter from a Mr. Jennings apropos of a recent fund-raising letter we'd sent out.

I didn't have a clue who James Harold Jennings was, and he was clearly pissed off (and maybe kind of crazy??), but I had very recently had a long phone conversation with *Bluegrass Unlimited*'s Pete Kuykendall, and in the course of that conversation Pete said something about

FROM JAMES HAROLD JENNINGS
RI PINNACLE NC 27043
BOX 5580
I WISH YOU TO UNDERSTAND THAT I SENT YOU A CHECK
FOR THE OLD TIME HERALD = AND I HAVE NEVER
GOT THE FIRST ONE = HOW IN THE HELL
DO YOU EXPECT TO GIT ANY CONTRIBUTIONS
FROM PEOPLE - WHIN YOU THE
OLD TIME MUSIC GROUP - WILL TAKE AND CASH
PEOPLES CHECKS
AND NEVER SEND THEM THE OLD TIME HERALD
THEIR IS MANY RADIO STATEIONS
I WILL GO BACK TO ROCK AND ROLL MUSIC
AND THE HELL WITH THE OLD TIME MUSIC
AND I CAN ALSO PICK A GITAR =
IF I WISH TO LISTEN TO OLD TIME MUSIC
I CAN PICK MY OWN GITAR
THE HELL WITH WPAQ RADIO STATEION
IF THEY WORK FOR THE OLD TIME
HERALD MUSIC GROUP. IF I DONT GIT WHAT
I PAID FOR YOU OR NO BODY ELSE WILL
HEAR OLD TIME MUSIC AGAIN AROUND
MY PLACE = SO LETS ROCK AND ROLL
FROM JAMES HAROLD JENNINGS
R1 BOX 558D
PINNACLE NC 27043
THE HELL WITH THE OLD TIME MUSIC ← ROCK AND ROLL
BABEYS. COME ON SUGAR LET US ROCK AND ROLL

HI STRANGERS
MY NAME IS JAMES HAROLD JENNINGS
RI BOX 558D PINNACLE NC 27043
I SENT YOU A CHECK ON THE DAY OF
FEB 24 1989, FOR THE OLD TIME HERALD.
AND AND I HAVE NEVER GOT THE
OLD TIME HEARLD
THE CHECK HAS RETURNED TO ME.
THE CHECK HAS BEEN CASHED.
ON THE BACK OF THE CHECK IS SAYS
FOR DEPOSIT ONLY
THE OLD TIME MUSIC GROUP. INC
THE OLD TIME HERALD
PO BOX 1368
GALAX VA 24333
CASHED IN MARCH 89
ON THURSDAY APRIL THE 6TH I GOT A NOTICE
FROM THE OLD TIME HERALD MUSIC GROUP
TRYEING TO RIP ME OUT OF MORE MONEY
GIT THE OLD TIME HERALD TO ME
OR SEND MY MONEY BACK —
I HAVE GOT MY CHECK IT WAS CASHED
AT THE DOMINION BANK
AND YOU CAN BET I WILL KEEP THE LAST
NOTICE YOU SENT ME TO USE AGAINST YOU
IF WPAQ RADIO STATEION WORKS
FOR PEOPLE LIKE YOU I WILL TURN
THEM OVER TO THE FCC

THE OLD-TIME HERALD
P. O. Box 1362
Galax, Virginia 24333

703-236-7808
703-236-9249

April 12, 1989

James Harold Jennings
Rt 1 Box 558D
Pinnacle NC 27043

Dear Mr Jennings,

We received both your letters expressing your concern about not having received your OTH yet.

We checked our records and indeed we have your card on file and also on the computer. It lists your expiration date as 11/89, which means you should have received the spring (Feb-April 1989) issue as your first one. Obviously something got fouled up on our end and we apologize. We are not out to rip anyone off. Sometimes things get mixed up at the post office's end too.

Please find enclosed the spring issue of the OTH. The next issue (summer - May-July) will be mailed out at the end of April and you should be getting it toward the beginning of May. If you have further trouble please let us know, or check with your post office. There may be a problem at that end.

We hope you don't go over entirely to rock and roll.

Very best wishes,

Alice Gerrard, editor

keep

FROM JAMES HAROLD Jennings
R1 BOX 558D
PINNACLE NC - 27043

HI FOLKS I AM VERRY HAPPY NOW.
ON Wednesday APRIL 12 I GOT
MY FIRST OLD TIME HERALD
I WAS VERRY GLAD TO GIT IT.
And I WISH TO Keep IT comeing.
NOW I CAN send YOU A CONTRIBUTION
PLEASE Remember ME And
Keep The old Time HERALDS comeing
And LET me Know IF I CAN GIT
ALL The EARLY COPYS -
That I did NOT GIT = LeT me Know
HOW MUTCH money TO send TO GIT
The LAST YEARS COPYS
I Am sending MY CONTRIBUTTON
one Hundred DOLLARS

A once-in-a-lifetime experience: A series of letters between subscriber James Harold Jennings and the *Old-Time Herald* in 1989.

the customer always being right, and even if you were mad, you should take that into account in your dealings with disgruntled subscribers. So I sent Mr. Jennings a conciliatory letter.

When Mr. Jennings replied, in addition to a one-hundred-dollar contribution, he sent a photo of himself with the words "James Harold Jennings, visionary artist" scrawled on the back. I was determined to look Mr. Jennings up and managed to locate him living in a school bus near the side of a road in Stokes County, between Winston-Salem and Mount Airy. There were two buses; he lived in one and kept all sorts of art materials in the other. He had a battery radio over which he listened to radio station WPAQ in Mount Airy, known for its religious programming but also for its many wonderful daily programs of old-time music, both recorded and live. We chatted a bit; he talked about his love for old-time music; he showed me around his place, showed me his art and what he was working on, and we had a sweet hour or two. (While I was visiting Jennings a black limousine-type car pulled up, disgorging a couple of New York art people there to check on Jennings, as he was soon to have an exhibit in New York City.)

I had brought neither a camera nor a tape recorder with me and didn't buy any of Jennings's work while I was there, which I regret. In those days, and to some extent now, I often felt that when visiting someone for the first time it was better not to have a tape recorder or camera—save those for subsequent visits. I wanted to be present in the moment, get to know the person a bit. But as it turned out that was the only visit I had with him, and as noted on the American Visionary Art Museum website, Jennings's "impending fear of the future drove him to suicide on his 69th birthday." So I regret that I didn't take pictures or record him talking. You never know.

Fortunately, Roger Manley had written a book, *Signs and Wonders: Outsider Art Inside North Carolina*, with some wonderful photographs he had taken of Jennings, one of which we featured in our Photo Bonus

FACING Virgil (1902–97) and Mabel Anderson, 1989. They lived on the far side of Rocky Branch, Kentucky, in eastern Wayne County. Virgil, a virtuoso banjo player, singer, and guitar player, was heavily influenced by the Black music that he listened to as a young man, and he had a very bluesy style of playing and singing. His wife Mabel was a wonderful storyteller, especially of scary stories, and I remember visiting them once when she mesmerized me with tales of panthers ("painters") who would get on the roof, tear the roofing off, drop down into the house, and run off with small children. Near their home Virgil had tacked a sign to a tree that read, "Now entering Anderson's Corners, population 2, Virgil Anderson Mayor." This image was part of a bonus feature of back cover photographs of musicians reading the OTH. Included were, among others, John Hartford, Grandpa Jones, Ramona Jones, and Walker Calhoun.

The OLD-TIME HERALD

campaign. Photo bonuses were of mostly well-known (at least to the old-time music community) old-time musicians "reading" the *Old-Time Herald*.

Eventually, in about 2003, I wanted to turn my attention more to my music, and my friend and fellow musician Gail Gillespie agreed to take over the magazine for several years. She was followed by Sarah Bryan (at the time with the North Carolina Folklife Institute). In 2023 Sarah stepped down, and as of this writing she is in talks with various organizations regarding the magazine's future, and whether or not one of them might take it over. You might say the *OTH* is alive but in limbo, and no issues are being published at this time.

I wouldn't take anything for the *Old-Time Herald* days with all their highs and lows, aggravations, and delicious rewards. I learned so much and am forever grateful to all the folks who participated in its birth, in carrying it forward, in helping it to grow and change—and that includes the many faithful readers who supported the *OTH*, letting us know about their lives, their likes and dislikes, sometimes complaining, often praising, but who always kept it coming. . . . I'm forever grateful.

Another *Old-Time Herald* pitch involving visiting friends Hilary Dirlam (one of the original board members) as well as banjo player Al Hart (d. 2017) and fiddler Kerry Blech (d. 2023), both from Seattle. They are sitting on my three-quarter-ton truck in my yard in Galax, 1987.

EPILOGUE

In the mid-1990s I joined up with Tom Sauber and Brad Leftwich to form Tom, Brad, and Alice. Brad, originally from Oklahoma, was living with his wife Linda just outside of Mars Hill, North Carolina. I was visiting my friend Hilary Dirlam, who lived nearby, and Brad stopped by to talk with me about singing. He wanted to be a better singer and could we do some singing together. Yes, we could, and we did. I met Tom at an IBMA event (don't remember when); we did some jamming and I loved his music. Brad and I were at an early Clifftop (Appalachian String Band Music Festival). We were playing together and Tom strolled up and joined in with us. We liked what we did and how we sounded and decided to make a go of it. We toured a lot for about ten years and made four CDs. We were a really good old-time band, if I do say so. Both Tom and Brad were amazing fiddle and banjo players, and we put a lot of emphasis on singing as well as playing.

Wayne Martin introduced me to many traditional players within visiting reach of Durham—musicians like fiddler Lauchlin Shaw and his wife Mary Lily in Harnett County, banjoist A. C. Overton and his wife Ava near Raleigh, and fiddler Joe Thompson and his wife Polly over in Mebane. I visited as often as I could, joining in on jam sessions or enjoying a small session with one or two others, often staying for snacks or a meal. I'll never forget one visit to A. C. with my grandsons Adam and Josh (then eight-ish and ten-ish), who were huge lovers of all things fishing, as was A. C., who invited them over to fish in his well-stocked pond. Adam threw his line out and very shortly a fish took hold and dragged it out into the middle of the pond. Surprised, Adam dropped the pole and saw it disappear. We hollered for A. C.; he came out, calmly threw another line out, miraculously hooked the fish, and brought it in with Adam's pole and line still attached. That experience is still with those boys to this day, and the story gets told often. It was magic!

Tom Sauber (*in back*), Brad Leftwich, and me in one of our first band photos, ca. 1994. Photo by Gail Gillespie.

Joe Thompson standing by his garage in Mebane with his cousin Odell, ca. 1988–89.

Somewhere around 2010, I teamed up with Beverly Smith, a singer and instrumentalist I knew from her work with the Heartbeats and with Carl Jones. She needed someone to go with her on tour in Europe and a weeklong workshop in Spain. Who could say no? We performed for several years as a duo, made one CD, *The Cherry Tree*. In 2013, the Piedmont Melody Makers came into being to play and sing original material as well as traditional bluegrass and some old-time. The band was Chris Brashear, Jim Watson, me, and Cliff Hale. We all lived in the same area, which made it easy to get together and play and practice. We toured some, played local gigs, and had a big time. But when COVID came along, it changed a lot. Cliff moved to West Virginia and joined others of his family to form an anti-COVID bubble; Chris and his wife Betsy moved back to Amherst; so that kind of broke us up (though we talk of a reunion. . .). Between 2006 and 2017, I recorded two projects with my friends Gail Gillespie and Sharon Sandomirsky—*The Road to Agate Hill* and the cassette *You've Been a Friend to Me*. I joined up with Kay Justice to record *Tear Down the Fences* with guests Gail Gillespie, Mac Traynham, Ginny Hawker, and Joe DeJarnette.

Periodically between 1994 and the present day, I would gather material that I wanted to record as "solo" stuff. This included three CDs of traditional and original material, and one of all originals—*Bittersweet*, produced by my friend and fellow musician Laurie Lewis. My last solo CD, produced by M. C. Taylor, my former graduate student assistant at the Duke University Center for Documentary Studies, was nominated for a Grammy in 2015. Early in the morning, I got a phone call from Josh Rosenthal at Tompkins Square Records asking me if I'd ever been nominated for a Grammy. I said, "No," and he said, "Well, you are now!" At first, I wasn't of a mind to travel to L.A. and attend the Grammys, but friends talked me out of that mind, and I went out there with my brother, my daughter, and my grandson. We had a ball, dressing up, walking the red carpet, hobnobbing with other musicians and friends.

Piedmont Melody Makers. *Left to right*: Cliff Hale, Chris Brashear, me, Jim Watson, ca. 2016.

Me, Kay Justice, Gail Gillespie: The Herald Angels, ca. late 1990s. Photo by Bunny Medeiros; courtesy Alice Gerrard.

My recorded musical life kind of came full circle around 1997 while I was cleaning out a closet at home and found some old reel-to-reel tapes of Hazel & Alice practice sessions. As I listened to these forgotten reels, I realized they contained some gems, many of which we'd never recorded. Eventually they became *Sing Me Back Home: The DC Tapes, 1965–1969*—a project on Free Dirt Recordings released in 2018. By the way, my music is available on Bandcamp at alicegerrard.bandcamp.com.

I continue to play music with friends, have just finished a new recording project of original songs (mostly written during COVID), *Sun to Sun*, which was released in November 2023 on Durham's SleepyCat Records, and I'm working on this book.

As I said before, some of the most gratifying and rewarding little joys that keep coming back are the letters that people wrote mentioning an *OTH* article that profiled a family member and how much it meant to them. And such joys keep coming today. I recently received a letter (or maybe it was an email) sometime around 2022 from a relative of the

Parish family wondering if there were any more of the LPs that Andy and I made of Roscoe and Leone. As it happened, I had a couple, and I sent her one. She responded, "I can't begin to tell you how much I appreciated the album—brought tears to my eyes to hear Roscoe's fiddle and Leone's beautiful voice singing 'Ring the Bells.'" She enclosed a small jar of fig jam that she'd canned earlier that summer. "It's from a recipe I found among my grandmother's recipes," she told me, "and she had written 'from Ninnie and Leone at the Farm' on it—so it must have been a Parish favorite.—Jane Parish Rife."

I occasionally get requests from folks asking for photos of a loved one (usually a musician) that they would love to have a copy of. I love this.

And now, instead of wonderful children who need babysitters, I have a wonderful dog, Polly, who needs dog sitting if I go away. Like I said earlier, full circle. There were always dogs in my life and they are there still: as a child Scotty, Boomer, and countless adopted neighborhood dogs; as an adult, Ginger, Ebenezer, Dovey, Willie. . . . With Polly I've discovered another passion: teamwork in various sports like agility, and household chores like getting me a beer from the fridge, picking up her stuff and putting it in her basket, and picking up my stuff that I drop.

I was challenged recently to teach her to put the empty beer can into the recycling bin, so added that to her accomplishments. I once remarked to Beverly Smith, "How is it that I don't have kids living at home, so I get a dog with problems?" She said, "Maybe you needed a project."

Maybe.

ACKNOWLEDGMENTS

I would never have been able to get this book published without the help of so many friends who assisted me as best as possible with sometimes faded memories, made suggestions, corrected facts when necessary, and so on. It was generally a group project, and I can't thank them enough.

Besides Lucas Church, the readers, and all the other good folks at UNC Press are the following:

Heather Anne

Paul Brown

Andy Cahan

Bill Clifton

Kenny Dalsheimer

Marybeth Dugan

Bobby Fulcher

Philip Gerrard

Thomas Goldsmith

Tatiana Hargreaves, for her friendship and her hard work helping me digitize all my black-and-white negatives.

Murphy Henry

Michael Kline

Chester MacMillian

Marge Marash and her children, Kim, Arley (Chris), and Jeremy Seeger

Anya McGuirk

Ashley Melzer, for her good advice on a host of issues. I don't think I'd have made it through this book process without her help.

Gabi Mendick

Eliza Meyer

Claire Milliner

Nancy Dols Neithammer

Scott Odell

Penny Parsons

Tom Rankin

Jim Steele

Charlie Thompson

A'yen Tran, for helping me out with computer issues that would have otherwise driven me crazy.

Wanda Urbanska

My family, who weighed in when necessary

And to all my friends who helped with my dog, Polly: I'm so grateful for you, and so is Polly. It really took a village: Babs Brown and Lucy Harris and all their friends who walked, fed, and took care of her through the years. A big shout out also to those who introduced Polly and me to dog sports and were my teachers: Cindy Hensley, Lisa Brockmeier, Sue McKinney, Christina Tracey, and Baptist Knaven. And thanks to all Polly's and my doggy friends—you know who you are!